Comrades

www.penguin.co.uk

Also by Rosita Boland

Elsewhere: One Woman, One Rucksack,
One Lifetime of Travel

Comrades

A LIFETIME OF FRIENDSHIPS

ROSITA BOLAND

doubleday

TRANSWORLD IRELAND
Penguin Random House Ireland, Morrison Chambers,
32 Nassau Street, Dublin 2, Ireland
www.transworldireland.ie

Transworld Ireland is part of the Penguin Random House group of companies
whose addresses can be found at global.penguinrandomhouse.com

First published in the UK and Ireland in 2021 by Doubleday
an imprint of Transworld Publishers

Lines from *The Unbearable Lightness of Being* by Milan Kundera
(Faber & Faber) on p 52 reproduced by kind permission of The Wylie Agency.
Line from Philip Larkin poem 'This Be The Verse' from *Collected Poems*
(2003) on p 55 reproduced by permission of Faber and Faber, Ltd.
Line from Seamus Heaney's title poem to *The Haw Lantern*
(1987) on p 56 reproduced by permission of Faber and Faber, Ltd.
Lines from 'Snow' from *Collected Poems by Louis MacNeice* (Faber & Faber)
on p. 215 reproduced by kind permission by David Higham Associates.

Every effort has been made to obtain the necessary permissions with
reference to copyright material, both illustrative and quoted. We apologize
for any omissions in this respect and will be pleased to make the
appropriate acknowledgements in any future edition.

A CIP catalogue record for this book
is available from the British Library.

ISBN 9781781620540

Typeset in 11.5/15pt Electra LT Std by Jouve (UK), Milton Keynes
Printed and bound in Great Britain by Clays Ltd, Elcograf S.p.A

The authorized representative in the EEA is Penguin Random House Ireland,
Morrison Chambers, 32 Nassau Street, Dublin D02 YH68.

Penguin Random House is committed to a sustainable
future for our business, our readers and our planet. This book
is made from Forest Stewardship Council® certified paper.

1

For my friend Róisín Ingle
'Can't even.'

'Wherever you are, it is your friends who make your world.'

– William James

'Deep experience is never peaceful.'

– Henry James

Contents

INTRODUCTION

I WROTE MOST of this book in 2020, the strangest year in our lives for many of us. I was alone throughout the many weeks of lockdown, but also not alone, because I was writing about some of my many and varied friendships, and sometimes it seemed like these people were in the room with me. In the evenings, some of these friends appeared on the screen of my phone, as we FaceTimed and Zoomed with each other. I missed their real-life company so much.

My friends are my comrades. That's the word I've always used to describe them. I can't even remember when I first started using this expression. It's nothing to do with socialism. My *Chambers Dictionary*'s first two definitions of 'comrade' are:

> *A close companion.*
> *An intimate associate or friend.*

The third one is:

> *A fellow soldier.*

My friends have been all those things to me. Close companions. Intimate associates. Fellow soldiers. You can't choose your family, but you can choose your friends. As we go through life, we both gather and lose them. We make friends at school, college – if you are lucky enough to go – through work, or while travelling, or through sport, or any of the many things people do in groups. I have accumulated very many friends over the course of my life, and I'm not done yet. Sometimes I joke that my friend quota is full, but the truth is, there's always space for another smart, kind, funny, irreverent, interesting person in my life.

There are so many disparate kinds of friends. I wanted to try to explore some of those friendships. Friends we hope might become more than a friend. The one who is always there with wise advice and who never judges. The friends you met out on the road years ago, and who are still in your life. The friends we lost, who went away from us for reasons we still don't understand. Then there are the friends who died, but whom we never forget.

Not all the comrades who appear in this book are human. As a child, I had an imaginary dog and two imaginary play-mates. My most important friendships back then were with books and the characters I read about in them. Books will always be my friends: the new, as yet unread, undiscovered ones, and those that I read years ago, and whose stories shaped my life.

There is always natural attrition with some friendships. None of us has every friendship from every time in our lives for ever. They come and go. Sometimes we just grow away from people. Or geographic distance eats away at the friend-ship, until one day, there's nothing left. Or it somehow becomes an effort, instead of a joy, and although friendships can endure many challenges, I now know they become stone-cold dead when they are an effort to maintain.

William James was an American philosopher and psychologist, and the brother of novelist Henry James, who turns up at the very end of this book. He lived from 1842 to 1910 and was as pithy and memorable in his quotes as the master of that particular art, Oscar Wilde.

'The greatest weapon against stress is our ability to choose one thought over another.'

'Actions may not always bring happiness, but there is no happiness without action.'

But my favourite quote of all from William James is this one:

'Wherever you are, it is your friends who make your world.'

It's my favourite, because it speaks to me. It's true. My friends are especially important to me because I don't have children, although I very much wanted to. Or – not right now, anyway – a partner. My friends make my world. They are family to me. Modern families are composed of more than shared DNA. When you don't have children or a partner, a significant portion of your time is spent with friends. They are very important in your life or, certainly, my closest friends are extremely important to me. They are all essential in different ways, and I am simply grateful these people continue to want to be my comrades.

I think the pandemic made many of us reassess certain things in our lives. How and where we spend our time, both at work and at home, and who we spend that time with. When

I couldn't travel abroad or see anyone for weeks and months at a time, the people I most wanted to be with came sharply into focus, and most of them were my friends.

As William James wrote, 'Wherever you are, it is your friends who make your world.' And my world was the lesser for a time for not being able to see the people who make it.

IMAGINARY FRIENDS

IN THE BEGINNING, I had no friends.

'Will you be my best friend?' I asked another small girl at the school I attended, as we were walking in the playground one afternoon, carefully balancing on the raised kerb that marked the boundary between grass and tarmac. I had no idea what a best friend was, except it seemed important to have one. Everyone else did. They linked arms, and swapped doll's clothes, and lined up behind each other after break, before going back into class again. They were self-contained units of two, who mixed with other units of two, and who chose each other to be on their team in games. I was not a unit of anything.

There was a pause. I didn't even like this girl, but I liked being on my own in the playground even less. Please say yes, I thought. Maybe this time, someone will say yes.

'No,' she said, staring at me with a sense of triumph, a knowledge of power that was innate, understanding she had something I wanted. We were seven. 'I already have a best friend.'

So too did the other girls I asked – we were an all-girls convent school – so I eventually gave up asking. Besides, what I really craved at that point in my life was not a human friend but a canine one. I wanted a dog.

I wanted a dog and it was impossible because my father did

not like dogs, did not ever want to have a dog in the house and would not entertain the notion of domestic dogginess for a second. This was a terrible problem because I really, really, really wanted a dog.

We all have some heart's desire as children, and mine was a dog. I wanted a shadow creature to follow me around and adore me unconditionally. His coat would be black and furry and his tail always wagging. He would sleep on my bed. He would wait for me to come home from school and run out the instant the gate opened. I planned to teach him tricks. I faithfully watched *One Man and His Dog* on Sunday afternoons for tips. The collies flew around the fields, pressed down against the grass, swift and fluid as water. Their owners did mysterious things with whistles, their dogs herded sheep with flabbergasting accuracy and the connection between them both was what I absolutely longed for.

In the days when I believed implicitly in magical thinking, I used every opportunity to wish for a dog. A proportion of my reading involved unquestioningly accepting otherworldliness of various kinds. Whether it was the grumpy sand-fairy Psammead in Edith Nesbit's *Five Children and It* that granted wishes; or stepping into a wardrobe and discovering Narnia lay beyond, as in C. S. Lewis's *The Lion, the Witch and the Wardrobe*; or the near-fantastical arrival of the three Fossil children, as gathered by Great-uncle Matthew in Noel Streatfeild's *Ballet Shoes*, my boundaries between reality and fantasy were slightly blurred.

Besides, my mother often told me a story about how, when she was a little girl, she had seen a leprechaun. He was smoking a tiny pipe, at the farm gate at the corner of the field where the sheep were, and he vanished right after she glimpsed him.

She told me the story so often, and in such detail, that it was perfectly vivid to me. When people said leprechauns did not exist, I knew they were lying. And because leprechauns existed, it was perfectly reasonable to believe other unusual things to also be true. I was disappointed to have never seen a leprechaun myself, but then again, we did not live on a farm in rural Ireland, where it was easier to hide. They probably liked the countryside better than towns.

I did not absolutely know that Narnia lay beyond the clothes that hung in a wardrobe. True, the surreal and snowy land did not, for instance, appear when I tried walking confidently into the back of my own large wardrobe, resulting only in a bruised forehead, but, I reasoned to myself, why would it? The portal into Narnia lay elsewhere, through a different wardrobe. The fact was, magical things happened in the books I read – and I was always reading – so why, I decided, shouldn't they happen to me too?

Thus, I snapped chicken wishbones, and when I got the larger piece, I wished for a dog. I wished on new crescent moons; wishes that only counted when the new moon was first seen outdoors, with no glass between it and your fervent yearning. In our household, on the first of each month, if you incanted, 'Coinín, coinín, coinín bán,' three times before you spoke a word to anyone that day, you had a wish – or so my mother told me and, obviously, she knew everything. I faithfully incanted a mantra about these white rabbits each month and wished for a dog. I stirred Christmas puddings and wished for a dog. I blew out birthday candles and wished for a dog. As instructed, I did not tell anyone my wishes, because then they would not come true.

My longing for a dog resulted in a peculiar skill. I discovered

I had only to listen to a dog barking to be able to perfectly replicate the sound. I imitated happy-sounding barks, angry ones, doleful ones, excited ones, and could soon tell from the sound of the bark whether the dog was large or small. I stood at our gate and barked in friendship, and dogs came out of their nearby gardens to me. They put their paws up on the gate and licked my hand. I petted their heads and we growled playfully at each other. To this day, I can startle anyone by an unsettling and uncanny ability to produce the sound of a barking dog in any mood you care to name.

We went away somewhere in Kerry one winter weekend and, on the Sunday, attended Mass in a church new to us all. My mother announced in the car on the way home that being in a new church meant we could all have three wishes. Delighted by this hat-trick of aspirational bounty, I upped my wish list significantly. The unwelcome thought had begun to occur to me that my wishes were not, in fact, working.

As I sat in the back of the car on the way home, I earnestly wished yet again for a dog. But this time, because I had three wishes, I knew it was finally going to happen. The second wish was, I wanted the dog to be waiting at the gate for us on our return. It was my job to get out of the car at the beginning and end of journeys to open and close the gates at the top of our long driveway, so clearly that's where I would find the dog. The third wish was that my father would not object to the arrival of the dog. Not entirely sure of the kilowatt power of wishes in this regard, I spent the rest of the journey devising a plan to conceal the presence of the dog that would be waiting faithfully for me at our gate.

It was dark when we got home. I got out of the car, opened the gates and waved the car on, as usual. I closed the gates carefully, then looked around, under the glow of the orange streetlight.

'Here, boy!' I called confidently. 'Good dog!'

No dog appeared.

'Here, boy! Good dog! Come here, now!'

I spent several awful minutes searching through the damp-smelling trees and undergrowth on both sides of the gateposts, brushing fir boughs out of my way. I searched on until I got very cold, unwilling to believe the breakdown between the transmission of my heartfelt wishes and the magical thing that was supposed to happen as a result. Did I cry? Oh yes. I certainly did. I stood by the gateposts among the fir trees in the orange-tinted dark and sobbed, my fists in my eyes. Not just for the dog that was supposed to be there, but for the bitter realization that wishes did not work, even when you specifically directed them all to one source, with the hope that numbers would increase their power.

I stopped wishing for a dog after that. Instead, I imagined one.

Sky was not the dog I had wanted, but he was going to have to do, because he was the dog that arrived. I could not show off his tricks to anyone, because his sole audience was me. He jumped through a hoop my arms made, obediently gave the paw and rolled over to have his stomach rubbed.

I did not know what dogs ate, so I covertly fed him scraps under the table at dinner time. His coat was not black or shaggy, as I had longed for. It was a kind of pale sandy brown, and smooth, not textured. But he was warm under my hand and had lovely silky ears he liked me to pull gently, and he was my dog.

Sky did indeed follow me everywhere, except into the

bathroom, which was the only door in the house with a lock on it. I thought it was better he didn't see me while I went to the toilet: I didn't want anyone to see me on the toilet, even my dog. I always wondered why the books I read never mentioned anyone going to the toilet. The Famous Five and Swallows and Amazons were always having adventures camping outdoors, where there were definitely no toilets, but how they coped and where they went, I never knew.

Aside from my bathroom visits, Sky kept close by at all times. I discovered to my disappointment that he preferred to lie on the floor beside my bed, instead of on it, although I kept encouraging him to jump up. Sky did, however, put his head on my feet every evening when I was reading on the couch in the living room, my father unaware of the forbidden canine presence. Outside of Christmas, there were usually just four of us there: Sky, me, my mother and my father.

Mostly, I read every evening, but sometimes I played board games. I had learned to play Monopoly and Snakes and Ladders and Cluedo from my three siblings; all older and gone away either to boarding school or into their adult lives. I would set up the board on the little table I did my homework on and play by myself. It was easy to play Snakes and Ladders; I just chose my favourite counter (a red glass bead from a broken necklace), shook the dice twice over and was always scrupulous about keeping to the toss of the dice with the other turn, even when I was losing. It was much trickier to play Cluedo by myself and, obviously, Sky, being a dog, could not participate in the game: his job was to lie there under the table with his head on my feet, as usual.

But Monopoly worked out just fine with one and was the game I played by far the most. I was the red glass bead, and then I set up three other players, who represented my absent siblings. I threw the dice by turn for us all and made my property decisions for the four of us based on my own choices. I did not win that much: the dice kept it fair, as you never knew when you'd land in Jail, passing Go and forfeiting £200, or pick up a mean Chance card.

Eventually, my dog Sky faded away. It became harder and harder to find him in the room, to feel his head on my feet when I was reading at night or playing Monopoly by myself. His tail stopped wagging. He wasn't happy. He could never bark; he always had to be quiet. He was lonely when I went to school, having to hide from everyone else in the house. One day, I woke up and he was gone. I looked everywhere, but he never came back.

I was sad but also surprised to discover I did not feel the same grief at the disappearance of Sky as I had at the non-appearance of the dog I had once fully expected to find waiting for me at the gate.

The greatest joy of my childhood was reading. The day that I experienced the catalyst moment of suddenly understanding how to read, that process of actual transformative magic, when the mysterious small black things on the pages suddenly shifted into focus and made sense, and became words, sentences, stories, is one I recall with piercing clarity. In retrospect, the day I learned to read was easily the happiest and most joyous of my entire childhood.

Once I could read, I started to acquire the books which became my default armour against loneliness. Books were my friends and so too were the many characters I met within their pages. There were the books I inherited from my siblings.

There were the books already in the house, belonging to my parents. There were the books I bought: I asked for book tokens at birthdays and Christmas. There were the weekly four-or-six library books, depending on which librarian I presented four tickets for six books to: books I was always sad to return; I reread books so often, I preferred to have my own copies, and still do.

I read everything by Enid Blyton, the Adventure series being my favourite: the Castle, Sea, River, Circus, Mountain, Island, Ship and Valley of Adventure. I read all of Jennings. All of Just William and Billy Bunter. I read the Bobbsey Twins, Nancy Drew and Hardy Boys series. I read Hitchcock's Three Investigators series. I read my brothers' *Eagle* and *Shoot* and *Hotspur* annuals. I read the *Girls' Crystal, Diana, Mandy, Bunty* and *Jinty* annuals, as well as the *Beano, Topper* and, my favourite, *Whizzer and Chips*.

I tried the sprawling Chalet School series several times, but it didn't engage me. I read the Ballet for Drina series, and Lorna Hill's Sadlers Wells ballet series. I read all of Ruby Ferguson's Jill's pony books. I read the Professor Branestawm series and the Doctor Dolittle series.

There was one Tintin book in the house, *Red Rackham's Treasure*, which I read over and over and over, delighting in the wonderfully detailed drawings. Our library didn't carry any of Hergé's books, and the hardcovers – they only came in hardcover, that I could find anyway – were too expensive to buy when I could get three other books for the same money, so I was an adult before I read the rest of Tintin. I read Teddy Robinson and the Milly-Molly-Mandy stories and Mrs Pepperpot and Pippi Longstocking. I read all of Laura Ingalls Wilder and the Swallows and Amazons series and every Noel Streatfeild and Edith Nesbit book I could find. I read the Borrowers out of sequence, as I did the Chronicles of Narnia. I loved Frances Hodgson Burnett's A *Little Princess* quite a bit more than her *The Secret Garden*. I was amazed and not best pleased to discover that Anne Shirley of Green Gables grew up and got married in further books in the series.

I read Oscar Wilde's *Complete Fairy Tales*, and fairy tales by the Brothers Grimm and Hans Christian Andersen. Some fairy tales made me feel both thrilled and anxious, like *The Steadfast Tin Soldier*, who, despite his marvellous adventures and valour, ends up being melted in the fire along with his paper ballerina love. And some, like *The Happy Prince*, made me cry: the generous Prince and the gallant swallow who die together, the Prince's broken lead heart lying beside the dead bird on the city's dump. Still, I could not stop rereading these troubling fairy tales: reading them was a kind of lovely, predictable pain; like lowering myself slowly into a too-hot bath every Saturday night.

Like a beaver gnawing through logs, I got through all these books with efficient speed. I could read a book in half a day, and frequently did.

Somehow, astonishingly, I never came across any Roald Dahl. Nor Lucy Boston and her Green Knowe stories. Nor anything by Judy Blume. I only read Antonia Forest's challenging, thoughtful and thought-provoking Marlow school stories as an adult. It was the same with Dodie Smith's simultaneously charming and absolutely bleak *I Capture the Castle*. So too with Susan Cooper's mesmerizing The Dark is Rising quest series, which I definitely would have reread frequently as a child.

Philip Pullman's glorious His Dark Materials series was

still unwritten and far in the future, as was Meg Rosoff's transcendent *How I Live Now*, books I adored when I read them as an adult but wished so much I had had in my life when I was a child. In the future too were Harry Potter, Lemony Snicket, Horrid Henry and the many others I was to later borrow from the bookshelves of my nieces and nephews.

After a while, there began to be a similarity on the spines of the books that came to live on my shelves: Puffin logos. Some of the puffins were small and tubby, but most of them were upright, with heads almost as large as their bodies. I discovered that the tubby puffins belonged on the books that were older, usually those I had inherited from my siblings.

On every flyleaf, over the description of the book, were two identical lines. The first was 'Puffin Books', in capitals. Underneath, in a type I later knew to be italics, were the words, 'Editor: Kaye Webb'.

Before the story proper began, there were sometimes dedications, which I loved. I studied these dedications at the beginning of the book carefully, little clues left by the writer to other untold elements of the story.

'To Oswald Barron. Without whom this book could never have been written. *The Treasure Seekers* is dedicated in memory of childhoods identical but for the accidents of time and space.' This was in E. Nesbit's *The Story of the Treasure Seekers*. The narrator of the book was called Oswald, and I was both envious and entranced. Not only did this lucky, lucky person have a book written for him, but the main character also had his name.

'To Lucy Barfield. My Dear Lucy. I wrote this story for you, but when I began it I had not realized that girls grow quicker than books. As a result you are already too old for fairy tales, and by the time it is printed and bound you will be older still. But some day you will be old enough to start reading fairy tales again. You can then take it down from some upper shelf, dust it, and tell me what you think of it. I shall probably be too deaf to hear, and too old to understand, a word you say, but I shall still be your affectionate Godfather, C. S. Lewis.'

This was the dedication for *The Lion, the Witch and the Wardrobe*. It was one of my very favourite books and, as a result, I envied Lucy Barfield even more than I did Oswald Barron. She not only got this wonderful dedication, but one of my most beloved characters of all – brave, resourceful, kind Lucy – was named after her. And C. S. Lewis was her godfather.

The more dedications I read, the more puzzled I was when some books had none. *Tom's Midnight Garden*, by Philippa Pearce, a book I loved deeply, carried no dedication. Nor did *Ballet Shoes* by Noel Streatfeild, or *The Long Winter* by Laura Ingalls Wilder. It seemed extraordinary to me that someone could write an entire book and not think about whom to give the gift of that finished book, their names immortalized at the start of every story, there to see for whoever thought to look.

The midnight garden Tom finds each night the summer he is exiled via illness to an aunt and uncle who live in a flat where there is no garden is a triumph of imagination in every way. The grandfather clock in the communal hall strikes thirteen, Tom goes downstairs to investigate and opens a door he has been told leads only to a yard with bins. But what he sees when he opens the door after the clock has struck thirteen is a vast garden, with many trees and flowerbeds and a greenhouse and lawns. He goes back every night after that, and I was right behind, slipping unnoticed through the door alongside him.

Why had Philippa Pearce not dedicated her book about

Tom, the time-shifting garden in all its years and seasons, and Hatty, his essential friend when he had no others, to someone? I loved that book so much, with its beautifully plotted, intricate story, which wove together generations, dreams, time and the lives of the two lonely children at its centre. Every time I read the exquisite penultimate chapter, 'The Apology', I wept. I knew what imagination could create. I knew what longing for a companion felt like. I knew that people were really like trees: cut them open and you could tell their age by counting the rings within.

Because I reread my books so often, I knew them intimately. I especially loved to scrutinize the covers of my books. They were the only colour elements, with drawings on both front and back covers, sometimes making one big picture when you opened the book flat, which also meant cracking the spine, which I didn't like doing.

My Narnia Chronicles had come from my oldest brother, a magnificent box set, which I was always privately afraid he might someday want to reclaim. The cardboard box for the set was already broken when it came to me, but I didn't care; I loved it. It was the only box set I had, or had ever seen. There were drawings of a golden Aslan's head on a red background top and bottom of the box and Reepicheep from *The Voyage of the Dawn Treader* on the back with a cerise-pink feather, one of my favourite characters. There were black silhouettes of other characters and the illustrator's name, Pauline Baynes.

Pauline Baynes had done the cover artwork for all seven books, as well as the wonderful, atmospheric drawings inside. Polly and Digory – Digory! What boy was ever called Digory? I thought with amazement every time – hold tight to Fledge as the winged horse flies far above pale green valleys and forests in *The Magician's Nephew*. Prince Caspian in his sky-blue jacket on his glorious black horse gallops through a dark forest.

The cover of *The Last Battle* disturbed me greatly. The book was my least favourite, as was the cover artwork. The cover glows a kind of orange colour, with rusty browns, and there are swords and a fire and creatures who looked like they were in pain, and probably were, because they had just been stabbed. It made me feel peculiar and uncomfortable and downright scared to look at it.

At the back of my Puffins, along with short descriptions of other Puffin books, was this, on the last endpaper.

If you have enjoyed reading this book and would like to know about others which we publish, why not join the Puffin Club? You will be sent the club magazine, *Puffin Post*, four times a year and a smart badge and membership book. You will also be able to enter all the competitions. For details of cost and an application form, send a stamped addressed envelope to:

The Puffin Club Dept A
Penguin Books Limited
Bath Road
Harmondsworth
Middlesex

There was a black-and-white drawing of a jaunty puffin with a stamped envelope flapping in one wing. I read this ad, although I did not realize at the time it was an ad, over and over again, with every new book I read. I very much wanted to know all about the Puffin Club and, especially, to be a member of something. But there was one big, very large, problem.

I could not find out more about details of cost and get the necessary application form because that required me sending a stamped addressed envelope, and our Irish postage stamps were no good in England. And I did not know where I could find a British stamp.

Lucinda lived in the passageway between the house and the garage. The passageway was a long corridor between these two points. There were four doors off it, one to the kitchen, one to the large garage, and two more: the side door to the house, which family habitually used, and a back door to the back garden. The passageway contained a room with an extra toilet, which no one ever used except the workmen who occasionally arrived to do painting or gardening, and a scary dim room with a bare bulb that rarely worked.

We called this dim room the coal hole. It was where the aluminium bin and a gigantic mound of coal lived, and where a mouse ran over my hand more than once when I was filling the coal scuttle in the no-light. There was also a large space for bikes at one end, and other bits and pieces. All in all, the corridor, which had a surface of small, mottled blue-and-white tiles, was pretty long.

When I put my roller skates on in the evenings, Lucinda was always waiting in the passageway to skate with me.

'Coming skating?' she'd call, already with her skates on. She had short brown hair, a long red pinafore dress and a funny accent I couldn't imitate but recognized from television as American.

The roller skates I had were inherited from my sister. They were crude skates, adjustable pieces of metal attached between two sets of wheels. One size fitted all. There were leather straps that fitted over your shoes. They were far from elegant, and I was far from an elegant skater. What I really wanted to skate on was ice, and where I wanted to skate was down a frozen river to a place in England called Ely, like Tom and Hatty had done in 1895, but I lived in the wrong country and era for that.

I did not know anyone else called Lucinda. Several of my classmates were called Mary. There were also Bernadettes and Deirdres and Siobhans, and Theresas and Carmels and Geraldines and Mairéads, but definitely no Lucindas. Lucinda was the name of the character in *Roller Skates*, by Ruth Sawyer. At ten, she was older than me. Her parents had gone away for a year and she lived in New York City with people who were not relatives.

She had a pair of roller skates and skated around the city, making all sorts of friends and having all sorts of adventures. I envied her her roller-skating skills, and her freedom and her being American, which seemed particularly exotic to me. I especially envied her ability to find and make friends.

Lucinda also scared me. She had witnessed someone die, her friend Trinket, who had had some kind of unspecified malady. It appeared to have been some kind of mysterious fever. I didn't know what fever was. I had never seen a dead body, let alone witnessed anyone dying in front of me, and lingered over the pages recounting Trinket's oncoming death with a mixture of dread and curiosity.

Lucinda coaxes her own doctor to tend to Trinket, whose immigrant parents are too poor to call a doctor themselves. Trinket and Lucinda have a thing together: they sing. Or rather, Lucinda sings from books that were unfamiliar to me called the *Saint Nicholas Song Book* and *Water Babies*, and Trinket listens. Their special friendship song is 'Froggy would a-wooing go'. I had never heard this song and had no idea what it sounded like.

To be honest, the first time I read *Roller Skates*, like Lucinda, I did not understand what was going on either. The doctor wakes up Lucinda, where she is sleeping on a sofa in the same room, and says that Trinket is asking for her. What Trinket wants is 'Froggy'. As Lucinda sings, she thinks Trinket is falling asleep.

When Lucinda wakes early the next morning, Trinket's bed is empty. At first puzzled, Lucinda realizes the little girl, now well, has gone up to her own bed. The doctor takes her out for a walk and lets her chatter as they walk along by the Hudson River. Eventually, he draws her attention to the sea-gulls flying over the water.

'Do you know what the Eskimos believe about death?' he asked quietly.

'No.'

'They believe that when a person dies her soul becomes a white gull. You see, it is given wings, to fly hither and yon, where it wills, free as a bird.'

It was then that the terrible realization struck both myself and Lucinda. Trinket was dead! She was now an Eskimo-bird! Lucinda had been singing at a deathbed!

I would skate up and down the corridor, chattering away to Lucinda as I skated, telling her about my day. It was twelve left-right swoops of skate from the kitchen door to the garage door, and I went out most nights after dinner for half an hour or more, until it got too cold: even in summer, the passageway was cool, and in winter, I could see my breath. I couldn't skate in the garden, as the parts that weren't lawn were tarmacadam, not a surface my skates could get purchase on. Besides, Lucinda never appeared outside, only when I was in the corridor.

In all the nights we skated together, I found myself unable to ask Lucinda the things I most wanted to know. What did the 'Froggy would a-wooing go' song sound like, and might she sing it for me? I was extremely curious to hear the song, but what I really, really wanted to know was not the tune of the song.

What I most wanted to know was: what did it feel like to look at a dying person? I don't know what held me back. We chattered about so many other things, like the five dolls who lived in my doll's house, and which of us had had the most recent sighting of the mouse in the coal hole, and about the book I was currently reading, but I could not make myself ask that particular question, although I thought about it every time I saw Lucinda.

The skates were already handed down from my sister, and well worn. One evening, while I was putting them on, a leather strap broke. The skate was unusable. And one skate was no good to anyone. That was the end of my skating sessions. I suspected I wouldn't see Lucinda again, and I never did.

I was sad she was gone but also in some way relieved. It had been a struggle every time to try to unsuccessfully locate the courage to ask what seemed like such a dangerous question. Each time I had taken off my skates and gone back inside the house, with the question left unasked for another night, I felt with discomfort that I had failed to achieve something important.

It took me almost a year to find the single British stamp I needed to send off for the Puffin Club application form.

I asked everyone I knew. I sought that elusive stamp with patience, diligence and perseverance. It represented such a tiny sum of money but was also so seemingly utterly unattainable. I searched for that stamp like the Bastable children had sought their treasure; it was my own personal quest story.

In the end, I heard at school about someone's relatives coming to visit from England and, via an intermediary, I begged for a stamp to be bought in advance of the trip. Up until it was presented to me one break time, I did not know if it existed. I gladly swapped a fat bundle of comics for the precious, coveted, unfamiliar stamp with Queen Elizabeth's head on it and was finally able to send away for the Puffin Club application.

The letter that came back had 'The Puffin Club' in pink letters at the top, with the same jaunty puffin. Chairman: Kaye Webb. There it was again, the same name as was on the flyleaf of my Puffins. I read that it was a reading club for boys and girls who liked books. That a subscription of 75 pence for a year would mean four *Puffin Posts* would arrive through our letterbox and that the subscription also included an enamel badge, a set of book plates and a membership book. Moreover, members could enter competitions by sending stories, poems, reviews and jokes. 'If these are very good, we may print them in the magazine.'

It's become unusual again to get personal correspondence in the post but, back in the 1970s, children were not – or at least, I certainly was not – used to receiving any post. The thick envelope addressed to me that came through our letterbox sometime after I had sent off my 75-pence postal order was the most marvellous piece of post I had ever had. There was a white enamel badge of a puffin, like the ones on the book covers; there was a satisfying pile of book plates with a drawing of lion, unicorn and puffin, each one reading a book; there was a very small membership book with 'Private and Confidential' on the cover; and there was the magazine itself.

There was also a four-sheet newsletter of welcome, explaining how the club worked and who was who in the club, and who did what. There were photographs of everyone and short descriptions. Kaye Webb's entry read thus: 'Editor and club chairman. Our genuine nuclear reactor. Has more projects under way than the British Government and is a genius at finding just the right people to carry them out.'

On the front page, along with instructions about what to do about your subscription if you moved house and had a new address, was a piece about outings. I read that there were club parties and outings organized in school holidays. 'It's a club convention [I had to look up the word 'convention' in my grandmother's *Chambers Dictionary*] to go away from any meeting having made two new friends. So always bring a notebook and pen for exchanging addresses.' This was like reading fiction to me. I already knew I would never go to any of these outings or parties. They were all held in Britain.

I wore the badge; I glued the book plates into my favourite books and put my name on them; I hid the membership book in my bedroom where no one would find it; and I read the magazines so often I knew their contents as well as my books.

My membership number was 151781. I know that because I still have my membership book. There was a secret password too, and if you saw someone wearing a badge, or they saw your badge, the password was Sniffup – 'puffins' backwards. The response was Spotera – 'are tops'. Club outings and parties weren't possible, but surely I could not be the only member of the Puffin Club in Ireland? My Welcome newsletter had said: 'Wear your badge as often as you can and always talk to anyone else you see wearing one. It's a fine way of making new friends.'

I wore my little enamel badge hopefully so often, and always on our infrequent trips to Dublin, wondering if anyone would see it and utter the secret password of Sniffup to me, and then maybe I would make a friend, but no one ever did.

My *Puffin Posts* arrived four times a year, and the days they arrived were unfailingly thrilling. The covers, which always featured puffins, were marvels of colour and detail and humour. They always made me laugh out loud with pleasure. I loved the different typography fonts inside, although I did not know then what they were called, and everything about the design, layout and illustrations. I loved the interviews with writers, many of which were conducted by club members, the stories and puzzles and drawings and photographs sent in by members.

I tried to ignore the column called 'Branch News', which gave quarterly updates on what outings and activities lucky Puffineers in Exeter and Bolton and Glasgow and Bristol and Essex and many other places were doing. Almost worse were the reports from the annual 'Puffin Colony' holidays, where members between the ages of nine and thirteen – which was me – could go for a week, to some large house in the British countryside, and do all sorts of wonderful things together, and have authors come visit to read to them, and also to meet Kaye Webb herself, who I now knew was affectionately called Queen Puffin.

After four years of membership, I received another enamel badge in the post. This one had a black background. It was pinned to a card with the familiar jaunty puffin and the words:

'This badge has been specially struck for honourable four-year members of the Puffin Club.' I still have that too. I have everything.

Once a year, in London, usually in April, there was a Puffin Show that ran for more than a week. Writers went there and signed books and gave talks. There were displays of artwork by Puffineers, and photographs of them, and competitions, and all manner of glorious things. Admission was 10 pence, but 5 pence to Puffineers wearing their badges. I was almost sure of getting there one year, as I had been promised a week in London with my parents the year I turned eleven and before I went away to boarding school. We did indeed go to London for a week when I was eleven, but the two sets of dates did not match and so I never did get to go to a Puffin Show.

However, there were competitions in every magazine, and I entered some. I wrote poems and stories and posted them all off to the address in Bath Road, Harmondsworth, Middlesex. There was a regular competition for Odway's Ground, the continually running results of which took up two pages of the magazine. Odway was a philosophical dog who was always thinking about something odd. In each magazine, there were some words in a think bubble above Odway's head and the competition challenge was to write something inspired by these words. The words and phrases were satisfyingly strange and random: gold; sticky; perchance to dream; fire; too much weather; ye letter; aphid in ye pink rose; something broken, something neatly mended; revenge; water; bones.

I sent off a poem about bones, a six-line, ghoulish thing about the bones of a human body being pulled apart on a rack. To my absolute amazement and joy, when the next magazine arrived, there was my poem; published on Odway's page, with my name in bold underneath. It was the first time my name ever appeared in print, and not only that, but I was even paid for this poem. I received a postal order for 50 pence and a yellow cardboard certificate telling me I was being awarded Odway's DGM – the 'Dogstar of Great Merit'.

When I was fourteen, I decided to write to Kaye Webb, the Queen Puffin. I wanted to be a writer and she was the only person I knew who knew writers. I wanted advice. And so I wrote to her, sending the letter to the same address where I sent competition entries and my annual membership fee.

And Kaye wrote back to me.

Tom lived somewhere in the garden. He arrived into my life around the same time Lucinda departed and only appeared when I was climbing one of the three poplar trees located in a corner of the garden. There were other trees in the garden, but these were my favourites. They were in the most secluded part of the garden, apart from the trees in the overgrown field that lay beyond the house and was also ours, but the ground was too hillocky and the nettles too many and too high there to detain me long.

I would be in one tree, and Tom would appear and start climbing a different one. He could climb far higher than me, which annoyed me greatly. I was small and nimble, and the branches had grown out from the trunks in a kind of lattice shape, so two of the trees were easy to climb. I had a system about climbing each of the trees in turn, so that none of them would feel left out, although it was a fact that one tree in particular was not nice to climb: the branches were a bit too far apart for the length of my legs. I climbed far up each one, careful to keep close to the trunk, but at a certain point the branches became too pliant to take my weight. Tom, even though older and taller, had no problem shinning almost to the very top of every tree.

He loved to tease me, clinging on to the slender tree trunk and making faces down at me. He was company, but he often made me cross. For instance, he called me Four-Eyes, an expression I loathed. My chronic short-sightedness had only recently been diagnosed. One afternoon in the kitchen, my mother had asked me the time. I did not have a watch. Watches were something you got when you were no longer a child and so were less likely to lose or break these expensive items.

I had got off the high stool from the breakfast counter, where I was sitting with my book, and carried the stool to where the clock hung on the wall over the cooker. Then I carefully climbed up and stood balancing atop the high stool, as I always did when I wanted to know the time myself, peered at the clock, which was then eye-level to me, and told her. My mother had been reading the newspaper when she had asked the time and then, astonished, had put it down to watch me rearranging the furniture.

Until my mother pointed it out to me, I had had no idea this was not the usual method as to how people found out the time. It seemed completely normal to me, in the same way I had learned to misbehave at school so that I was regularly sent to stand in apparent disgrace beside the blackboard, in front of the class, to be stared at. It did not mean disgrace to me at all; to me, it was a practical way of being able to read something vital on the blackboard during class that I otherwise could not see. My desk was far away from the blackboard, the end desk by the wall on the right, in the back row of several rows in the very large classroom of forty-four other girls.

After the clock incident, I had been brought to an optician. My mother had asked the optician if too much reading could ruin a child's eyesight, and he, to my intense relief, had said no. When she asked the question, I had had a very horrible moment when I thought I might not be allowed to read any more. It turned out I just had very bad eyesight, like my sister and oldest brother. So now I could finally see what was written on the blackboard from the back of the classroom, but I also had ugly brown glasses with shamefully thick lenses and a nickname at school I detested.

'There's a great view from up here, Four-Eyes!' Tom would call down to me from above, in his tree, although I knew he was fibbing. The branches were too thick at that height to see anything much, unless you were perching on the top leaves like a bird, which he was not. The trees were close to the wall that ran around the large garden and where a public footpath lay on the other side. The people walking past along this footpath never once noticed me, secreted high above their heads. Neither did my mother ever spot me, on her way to the clothes line. Nor my father, when he came home from work, parked his car and went past me on his way into the house. I revelled in my magical invisibility. I couldn't get into Narnia via my wardrobe, but I could make myself invisible to adults.

Tom was English. I had never been to England. I had never been anywhere other than Ireland. He was not like Tom from *Tom's Midnight Garden*. He wasn't as interesting or thoughtful as the boy in the book about the magical garden that I loved. Besides, he didn't wear pyjamas, as that Tom did. My Tom wore brown shorts and a blue short-sleeved T-shirt with a collar, no matter what time of the year it was. He occasionally blew his nose with a cotton handkerchief he took from his shorts pocket, an item I had only ever seen used by my father. Never mind what we talked about. That was private business between us, and sometimes I learned things. But still, he annoyed me with his persistence. Whenever I started to climb one of those three trees, my mind went somewhere else and this frequently exasperating Tom appeared.

One summer's day, when the leaves were at their bushiest growth, I decided to keep on climbing up. I chose my favourite tree, the one in which I could already go the highest up into. When I reached my usual stopping point, I breathed in and kept going. As usual, Tom was already far above me, in a different tree.

'Careful!' he called down to me.

'I'm going to get up as high as you!' I called back with determination.

I kept on climbing, making sure to wrap one leg around the tree trunk at every new advance. The lattice of branches got smaller and more spindly and the trunk got thinner. Poplar trees are the giraffes of trees anyway, tall and thin and mobile, not fixed and substantial and solid like oaks or chestnuts, the elephants of trees.

'Four-Eyes, I don't think you should go any higher.' Tom had climbed down to meet me. He was in the opposite tree, exactly adjacent to me.

'One more branch,' I said stubbornly. I made the mistake of looking down. The little I could see of the lawn was far, far below, almost completely hidden by a thicket of leaves. Some people passed by on the public footpath on the other side of the wall, talking to each other. From the sound of their voices, I knew I was far above them. I swung myself up and, as I did so, the piece of the slender trunk I was holding on to carefully swayed and then simply bent sideways. I found myself falling. My glasses fell off. I think I screamed. I'm not sure. It all happened so fast.

Tom caught me. He had swiftly descended as I was falling, falling both downwards and sideways, into his tree. He grabbed me and the bent-over poplar and pulled me on to the branch where he was standing. Arms flailing, I tumbled on to and into the branch, and it held me. Winded, I stayed there for a bit, clutching the branch and the solidity of the tree trunk, breathing hard. When I looked around to reluctantly thank him, Tom was gone. I never saw him again.

Those poplar trees are all cut down now. The garden I played in, and the field where I did not, now have three more houses built within that same space. There is planning permission for one additional site and, in time, there will be five large houses on a site where once there was just one house, set in an extensive garden. The gateposts at the top of a long driveway where I once looked for a dog who was not there are not there any more. Nor are the fir trees, which I stood among alone that evening all that time ago and cried for the dog who was not there and for the wishes that had not come true.

The year I turned twenty-one, and before my final year in college, I lived and worked in London for a summer. I bought myself an A–Z and a travel pass and carried both of them everywhere. At some point, I wondered if Kaye still lived at the same address as the one she had given me when she had written back to me, seven years previously. She had ended her lengthy letter to me by asking me to write to her 'from time to time and tell me how you get on'. Would she still remember me? I wondered.

I sent a postcard with my temporary London address and, to my immense delight, back came a prompt reply. It was an invitation to call and see her on a Saturday afternoon. London had never seemed so full of riches to me as it did on that day. It wasn't just the museums and galleries full of wonderful things that I had been working my way through but the actual storied people, including the fabled Kaye, who lived there among the city's myriad streets.

On the appointed day, I bought yellow roses and set off for Maida Vale. There is a saying about never meeting your heroes, in case they disappoint. Nervously, I rang the bell. Nervously, I went up in the lift. Nervously, I knocked at the door with the number she had given me.

From the second Kaye opened the door of her gorgeous apartment overlooking the canal, I felt, in the oddest and most unexpected way, at home. She was in her seventies then and already had the debilitating arthritis that was to worsen as the years continued, but she in no way ever seemed old or unwell to me. Kaye was pure charm and verve and kindness. And always so hospitable. Her hair was in silver whorls and she welcomed me as if I was family, which in some way, I guess I was.

'Sniffup!' she incanted by way of greeting as I stepped through the door.

'Spotera!' I replied, my heart just about bursting.

I was finally chanting the secret password to someone who understood it, and not just to another member of the Puffin Club, but to the actual person who had created the entire thing: the password itself, the club that had given me so much joy as a child and the magazine that had introduced me to so many new books and authors. The person who had brought all those books to the Puffin list and thus given me the stories and characters and imaginary friends I had cherished so dearly.

Kaye's apartment was full of beautiful things: paintings, antiques, lovely furniture and hundreds, thousands, of books. We sat in the living room and talked for an hour. About books, mostly. She was still utterly tuned in to the children's publishing world she had retired from. She knew everyone. She had read everything. And was I still writing myself? she enquired. Why yes, I was. And did I know that her father, Arthur, had been a news editor on the *Irish Times*, and her mother, Ann, the theatre critic there? Did I know anyone at the *Irish Times*? I did not. I was still years away from joining the *Irish Times* myself and did not understand then what a news editor did, although I had a better idea about a theatre critic.

Along with the books on shelves, there were stacks and stacks of books on the floor, most of them newly published books that had come to her in the post. The tallest pile was all of the same book: a paperback anthology.

'Look,' Kaye said, putting one in my hand. 'These just arrived. Have one.'

The anthology was called *I Like This Story: A Taste of 50 Favourites*. Kaye had chosen them and written short introductions for each. It was the two thousandth Puffin Book to be published. There was a little banner at the bottom of the book, with '2,000th' in gold. To celebrate such a landmark for Puffin, they had gone back to her, the editor who had made the imprint so successful.

I opened the book. The dedication read: 'For all members of the Puffin Club, past, present and future.' I was finally included in someone's book dedication. It could not have been more perfect.

'Take it. But let me sign it for you first.' And she went off looking for a pen, while I opened the pages of this marvellous book, the Puffin to celebrate all other Puffins.

This is what Kaye wrote for me, back in the summer of 1986. 'For Rosita. The very first copy. To an ex-Puffineer, with love. Kaye (Webb).'

I carried the book back to the little flat in Borough that I was living in for the summer. When I went back to Ireland, I put it with all my old Puffin books and my *Puffin Posts*.

And of course I still have it.

There was more. Oh, there was more. I came and went twice more for extended periods of time to London during my twenties. During that time Kaye became a real, true and most definitely not an imaginary friend. She frequently hosted parties and afternoon gatherings and lunches at her Maida Vale apartment, and I went to everything I was invited to. It was there I finally met other members of the Puffin Club. We did indeed swap our names and addresses. One of the guests I met there, Hugo, a playwright a few years older than me, had illustrated several stories for the *Puffin Post* when he was in the club, illustrations that I remembered vividly.

'Please come to supper one day,' he said as I was leaving the afternoon soirée we first met at. I did not know anyone who called dinner 'supper', but I went anyway, to eat with him one evening in the rooms he occupied on the ground floor of a large old house by the Thames in Chiswick.

It turned out that it was Hugo who had run the Exeter branch of the Puffin Club and whose updates on club outings there I had read so longingly years before. Hugo had been many times to the Puffin Shows in London. He had in fact helped out and even stayed with one of the people who ran the Puffin Club; he knew everyone. He described the shows to me so well and told me in such detail about the things that had happened there that it was almost as good as if I had been at them myself.

Hugo and I became close friends ourselves and roamed all over London together at all hours of the day and night. He was, in fact, the nearest thing I have ever known to a human A–Z. He knew London intimately and was always showing me new marvels: Sir John Soane's Tardis-like museum-house in Lincoln's Inn Fields; the Whispering Gallery in St Paul's; Bunhill Fields, in whose graveyard William Blake was buried somewhere. Hugo's theatre contacts meant he could attend pretty much any play he wished for free, and he often asked me to come with him. I saw Ibsen's *Peer Gynt* and David Hare's *Racing Demon* at the National, and many, many plays at the Royal Court.

Hugo introduced me to Alexander, a Scottish friend of his, whom he knew from the time they had both toured with a show in the Highlands. The three of us became the tightest of trios for a period. One of the things we did together once a month was to bring dinner to Kaye's apartment. The three of us prepared a course each in the little kitchen, where I never failed to admire the antique blue-and-white Spode china on display, the cups of which we drank coffee from at the end of dinner.

Kaye's contribution to our monthly dinners in her home was providing the excellent wine, of which we drank an awful lot. The wine was always far better than our cooking, but she was much too classy a hostess to ever point this out. By then, Kaye was using a wheelchair. She was finding it harder to get out into the world. So the world, in the form of Kaye's many, many friends, including me, Hugo and Alexander – all three of us more than half a century younger than her – came to her at Maida Vale instead.

I loved those evenings when the four of us gathered around the table in the little dining room, talking non-stop, and Kaye telling the best stories of all. I did not notice Pauline Baynes's artwork for *The Last Battle*, that well-remembered depiction of an orange-glowing battle scene, the first time we all had dinner together in the dining room. That's because my back was to the glass cabinet, where the unframed illustration stood atop it, propped against a piece of china. It was only the next time the three of us were over and I was sitting at the opposite side of the table that my eye travelled upwards and I saw with astonishment the original cover artwork for one of the seven books in The Chronicles of Narnia.

'Pauline gave it to me,' Kaye said simply, when I asked. After that, I always made sure I sat on the side of the table where I could see the painting, which still, to be honest, disturbed me to look at. I didn't care that it was the cover illustration I had liked the least from the series of books I had loved so much. What I cared was that Pauline Baynes had created this cover illustration, and all the others too, including the detailed and atmospheric line drawings inside the books, all of them so familiar to me, as if they had been tattooed on my skin.

I was away travelling when the big party at the Victoria and Albert Museum was held to celebrate Puffin's fiftieth birthday. Hugo was there, though. He wrote to me to say that Kaye had made a speech about what being an editor and running the club had meant to her and, in the process, listed some friends she had made there over the years. Both Hugo's name and mine were called out that evening in the V&A. 'So you were there with us, even though you weren't there,' Hugo wrote to me.

I was, however, there in person for Kaye's eightieth-birthday party. A cream-coloured invitation with a delicate art deco border and, of course, the familiar, beloved little bird, arrived in the post from Puffin Books.

'Puffin Books invite you to a tea party, to celebrate Kaye Webb's 80th Birthday. At the Drawing Room, Claridge's, Brook Street, London W1A 2JQ, on Wednesday 26th January, 1994, from 3.30 p.m.'

This time, it was Hugo who was absent, away in the US, doing research for his latest play. I did not know what one wore to an afternoon tea party at one of London's grandest hotels but decided to dress up in honour of Kaye. I wore a long red crushed-velvet dress with a vintage black astrakhan jacket I had bought for a tenner in a market in Camberwell. I told everyone who looked at the fur disapprovingly that it was actually a wolf pelt, with important family connections.

'My grandmother shot the wolf from the Trans-Siberian train with a pearl-handled revolver. She made them stop the train to retrieve it. A furrier in Moscow made it into a jacket for her. Look, it has her initials inside.' And I would show them the black-and-gold embroidered initials of L.S., which were certainly someone's initials but definitely not those of either of my long-dead grandmothers, neither of whom had ever set foot in Russia.

The drawing room at Claridge's was full that January afternoon. The champagne glasses sparkled. There were white flowers everywhere and many people I did not know. Kaye was in the centre of it all, laughing with delight, her eyes shining as brightly as her silver hair. She always loved a good party and this was already a truly excellent party.

At some point, we were asked to sit down, to be served. We had been mingling with our champagne glasses, peering at each other's name badges, which we had been given on arrival. The long tables with immaculate white linen had name cards. I searched for mine, found it and then took my allotted seat. There was already someone sitting on my right side, an older woman. We turned to each other in greeting, our hands extended.

Her name badge read: Pauline Baynes.

On 17 December 1993, Kaye was Sue Lawley's guest on *Desert Island Discs*. I knew from Hugo she was going on but didn't hear it when it was originally broadcast. When I was writing this essay, I went online and looked to see if I could find Kaye's *Desert Island Discs* anywhere. In recent years, the BBC has been adding to its digital archive and you can now find very many old programmes that went out when airtime was analogue only. It took me under a minute to locate it on the BBC website; all those years since she was on air compressed like time travel, Kaye was both in the past and also in the present, like Tom and Hatty in their ever-changing midnight garden.

I didn't play the programme straight away. I waited a little while. I needed some time before I could go back in time and listen again to the voice of my beloved friend.

One of the pieces of music Kaye chooses is the 'Puffin Song', a jaunty, cheery affair that played in bookshops back in the day to promote the books. 'There's nuffin like a Puffin, nuffin like a Puffin book to read, there's so much in a Puffin, it's full of super stuffin' . . .' The song prefaces her reminiscences about working as a children's editor for twenty years and how she set up the Puffin Club in 1967.

'Nineteen sixty-seven, I think it was when you started the Puffin Club,' Sue Lawley says. 'Which won thousands and thousands of members very quickly, didn't it?'

'Yes, it did,' Kaye replies. 'They put my name on the books, which said, "Editor, Kaye Webb," so they [the children] had somebody to write to, and this is really what made me realize how important a club could be, because what they wanted was anybody, somebody out in the world outside, to whom they could write.'

I played that section back several times. It was as if she were talking directly to my childhood self. It was so exactly what I had wanted: somebody out there in the world to whom I could write. I don't know how many other people there are who, like me, once found a way out of profound loneliness by writing off for an application to the Puffin Club, but I cannot be the only one. I sat in my house listening to my friend talking about her life and felt such absolute gratitude for her vision and her editorship.

Kaye died two years after her party in Claridge's, almost to the day, ten days short of her eighty-second birthday. I was living back in Ireland by then. It was Hugo who told me the news, via letter, enclosing photocopied obituaries from various newspapers. I was living by the Atlantic at the time, in the west of Ireland. I put down the letter and went for a walk by myself to digest the news and grapple with the torrent of emotion it had provoked in me.

It was the end of January, a bitterly cold afternoon. The seagulls called and swooped over the water, as they once did in a story I read long ago when my roller-skating friend Lucinda realized that her friend Trinket was dead.

> *'Do you know what the Eskimos believe about death?'*
> *'No.'*
> *'They believe that when a person dies her soul becomes a white gull. You see, it is given wings, to fly hither and yon, where it wills, free as a bird.'*

I stood at the edge of the Atlantic and watched the seagulls ascend in the sky.

THE DESIRED FRIEND

FOR THE FIRST three years of my college degree, I rarely drank alcohol. In O'Neill's pub on Suffolk Street, the default pub for Trinity's English department at that time, I drank soda and lime while everyone else downed pints of Fürstenberg and Guinness. I wasn't interested in drinking during those years, but it was more than that. I was afraid to let go, to take a risk, or of who I might become if I drank like the people I knew, turning maudlin at the end of the evening and confessing to my infatuation with a man none of them knew.

Kit, the subject of my infatuation, was three years older than me, a student of architecture at Bolton Street. A few months before I arrived in college, one of my boarding-school friends had set him up as my blind date for our graduation dance. We were all due to meet up at a friend's house in Athlone prior to going on to the Prince of Wales Hotel. Kit was coming from Galway.

Kit arrived to the house wearing his grandfather's dress tails, white shirt and white cravat. He was tall and had a face that although not conventionally handsome was full of an animation that made you look at it twice, three times. He had a habit of occasionally fixing you with a piercing, questioning gaze, from which it was almost impossible to look away and which I noticed right away.

'Hello, you,' he said, smiling, leaning over to kiss my hand, like a character from a novel.

'Hello,' I said back, in disbelief.

I had been enthralled from the start by Kit's confidence and the unselfconscious way he inhabited the remarkable clothes that made him stand out among a roomful of rented tuxes, acrylic frilly shirts and bow ties that came undone between the soup and the turkey and ham. When we danced, I realized that not only could he dance effortlessly, but astonishingly so could I, once he was guiding me.

After the dinner-dance part of the evening was over, a group of us went to someone's house for a party. Kit and I lay in a corner of the room, murmuring to each other. He was drinking a can of beer, and I fretted quietly that he would get drunk: I had no idea what the tipping point between sobriety and drunkenness was, let alone what merriment was. He talked about Paris, where I had never been and where he was to spend the summer with his French girlfriend, whom I stoutly hated immediately. He called me a poet: the friend who had set us up had told him I wrote poetry. Nobody had ever called me a poet before.

'My poet friend,' he said, taking my hand, and between the lack of sleep and the adrenaline that had scarcely ceased thrumming through me since we had met less than twelve hours previously, I honestly believed I was dreaming.

The sun came up early, about 4 a.m., and Kit and I went for a walk in the nearby meadows, arm in arm. It was a beautiful blue morning and the birds were loud in the quiet meadows that would shortly be cut. I had never before seen the dawn come up and wondered that morning how it was I could possibly have missed such a vital part to the day: what else, I found myself wondering, had I been missing out on?

'Promise me you'll get in touch when you come up to Dublin in September,' Kit said as we walked along the Westmeath boreen, the sun beginning to gleam above the far end of the meadows.

'I will,' I said, staring as the sun slowly rose, shimmering pale as mother-of-pearl in the haze.

I had. Within a week of arriving for college, we had met again and at once established a close friendship that I found myself unable to adequately explain to anyone.

'Is that guy Kit your boyfriend?' people would ask me.

'No, we're just really good friends.'

Kit lived for a pittance in rent in a semi-derelict, vast house on what had once been Dublin's most famous and grandest Georgian thoroughfare, Henrietta Street. The street had been developed by banker Luke Gardiner in the 1730s, and at one point in its past the residents of its sixteen houses had included four MPs, four peers, an archbishop and two bishops. The houses soared overhead like cliff-faces, anchored at the street's end by the galleon-like bulk of King's Inns. The street itself was still cobbled.

Kit had access to a toilet, but there was no bathroom and no proper kitchen facilities. There was a hob and a sink in his room, but no fridge. To my knowledge, there was no heating anywhere in the house at all. His room, at the back on the ground floor, was cavernous. It had a marble fireplace, bare floorboards, original windows with wooden shutters, double-height ceilings and original cornices, including a still-perfect ceiling rose. The paint on the walls was in various stages of peeling and flaking away, revealing layers of different colours beneath.

He had built a bed on a platform in one corner and had his drawing board in another. The room was always freezing in winter, even when Kit lit the fire with wood from pallets he salvaged from nearby Moore Street Market. I thought it was the most marvellous place I had ever seen.

Kit spoke French, rode a Vespa and could not only cook brilliantly but loved to cook, unique among the other male students I knew. He made pottery as a side interest and was always sketching unusual shapes of bowls to try next. Full of restless energy, two or three nights a week he was out at the climbing wall at UCD. He periodically disappeared unannounced during term for weekends or whole weeks.

'Where were you?'

'Away climbing.' Or, 'Away skiing.'

Kit seemed so thoroughly independent to me, as if he was already far beyond student life. I held on to his friendship as if it was a life-raft that would help transport me across some unknown stretch of water to somewhere else.

My own accommodation on the other side of the city was a little two-bedroom flat on Ranelagh's Windsor Road that I shared with three other girls. The Victorian house had been converted into three bedsits and one flat. Our first-floor flat did not have a fireplace, or window shutters, or a ceiling rose. It had storage heaters, an electricity meter which took 50-pence pieces and the white chipboard wallpaper that was everywhere in Dublin house conversions in the 1980s: in our flat, it was also papered to the ceilings.

We had a shared food kitty and a shopping, cooking and cleaning rota. There was a payphone in the communal hallway that took 5-pence pieces and a landlord who called on Saturdays with a rent book. I liked my flatmates a lot but, compared to the storied romance of the Henrietta Street house, our Ranelagh flat seemed somehow troublingly conventional to me.

Two of my flatmates were studying architecture and the other one interior design. They were in class all day and stayed up all night every six weeks or so, working to deadline on their regular class projects, while swearing and drinking an inordinate amount of coffee. They made scale models and drew axonometrics and floorplans and sections and elevations. Their work was visceral and practical and visible.

By contrast to their full days of classes, I had, in my first year, ten contact hours a week and just six in my fourth and final year. There was a weekly tutorial, where we were meant to discuss the assigned texts we were studying. I rarely had the confidence to speak up or the conviction that I had anything remotely worth saying. I must have said something sometimes, but the only tutorial from four years I distinctly recall saying anything in was once asking an existential question about what was the point of all this work – of reading, of learning, of life – of just about everything, when we were all going to die anyway.

This lecturer kept me back a week or two later to gently interrogate me as to whether I thought I might be depressed or not. I knew nothing about depression when I was a student, except I had some vague idea that this mystifying, amorphous state was what had led Sylvia Plath to put her head in a gas oven. Mortified, I more or less ran out of his office.

My two subjects were Modern English and History. It did not take me long to realize that academia was something that was never going to come naturally to me. I read one fellow student's essay on a shared English assignment and marvelled at his ability to perform seemingly effortless and dazzling analytical gymnastics. He had received a First for this essay. My own attempts at essays hardly ever amounted to more than a collapsing backflip or a wobbling, graceless dash across a beam.

What did increasingly interest me were people, hints of the personal lives of those whose work we were studying. Whose work we were specifically being instructed to read, as if it existed in some autonomous zone, far distant from those who had written it.

One evening in the Lecky Library, I opened up an assigned book of literary criticism and did not get any further than the dedication. The book was written by a man – whose name, of course, I cannot now recall – and dedicated to a woman. The dedication included an epigraph from the seventeenth-century metaphysical poet Andrew Marvell, a line from his poem 'The Garden'.

I knew the poem: we had studied it in our first year. It has nine verses. The epigraph came from the last line of the sixth verse.

> Meanwhile the mind, from pleasure less,
> Withdraws into its happiness:
> The mind, that ocean where each kind
> Does straight its own resemblance find;
> Yet it creates, transcending these,
> Far other worlds, and other seas;
> Annihilating all that's made
> To a green thought in a green shade.

A green thought in a green shade.

Under the library's hard fluorescent light, I read that line over and over. It had not made an impression on me when we had studied the poem, but now, in isolation, the line glowed like an otherworldly emerald. What, exactly, was a 'green thought'? I wondered, stirred and afire. Better still, what was a green thought in a green shade?

And what sort of person must this woman be and what sort of extraordinary relationship must she and this critic have had? Because it was obvious: this is how he had viewed her and, more, he had written it as a dedication to all who read the book to see and guess at. I sat mesmerized in the Lecky that evening, wondering if I would ever be thought of as a green thought in a green shade to someone, and would that someone perhaps, perhaps, perhaps be Kit?

Although I was deeply uninterested in politics or matters of gender, I did register somewhere that the vast majority of the writers assigned to our courses were male. The women writers I liked most, I also noted, had unfortunately ended up dead well before they should have, some of them by suicide. The Brontës and their doomed lungs; Sylvia Plath, with her head in that gas oven; Virginia Woolf filling her pockets with stones and walking into the muddy River Ouse one afternoon.

I recall one lecturer telling us that George Eliot had run out of options as to what to do with Maggie Tulliver in *The Mill on the Floss*: that there was nowhere else Eliot could go to develop her as a character and thus had to kill her off. What about just living your life? I thought, baffled, at the back of the class. Was that not enough? Why was it that complex, unconventional, independent Maggie Tulliver had had to die by drowning before the book could end?

The house Kit lived in had been, in living memory, a tenement. When I went to visit one evening, Kit told me of the two old ladies, sisters, who had called to the door that afternoon.

'They said they used to live here, seventy years ago, when they were children, and asked if they could come in. They were from a family of nine and they used to live in my room.'

'This room?' I said, looking around, trying to imagine nine people in the space Kit occupied alone.

'They said around eighty people lived in the house altogether when they were here. Guess what they showed me when they came into my room?'

'What?'

Kit took my hand and led me over to a corner of the room. 'Look,' he said, pointing down to the floorboards.

I looked. I thought I knew every inch of Kit's room, but neither of us had ever before thought to investigate the place near the window where a small rectangular piece of the floorboard had been cut out. Kit bent down and carefully prised the piece of wood up with a knife. There was a small space beneath, like an empty box.

'That's where their mother hid money from their father.'

My other subject in college with English was History and I was specializing in Georgian Dublin. The classic textbook of that period was Maurice Craig's *Dublin 1660–1860*, first published in 1952. I had gone straight to the index to look for the entry on Henrietta Street.

> To walk up Henrietta Street today is a striking and saddening experience. Though it contains only some sixteen houses, they are of so palatial a cast that one easily understands how it remained the most fashionable single street in Dublin until the Union.

This evidence of the house's 250-year decline from grandeur to poverty was suddenly viscerally right there in front of us, beneath the floorboards in Kit's room. It was in the oral history of the story he had been told, that very day, by women who not only remembered what tenements were but who had lived in one: right here in this very house, in this room. I found myself so moved I couldn't speak. I squeezed Kit's hand tightly and he squeezed it back, even tighter.

One Saturday morning, when I was around at Kit's for coffee, there was an energetic banging at the front door. None of the other tenants appeared, so Kit went to answer it. I heard the front door open and people come in, carrying something that sounded heavy when it thumped to the floor.

'Patrick!' Kit shouted. Patrick was the upstairs tenant, a fellow classmate from Bolton Street. When no Patrick answered, Kit ran up the stairs to knock on his door. I went out into the hall. There were two men standing inside the front door, a stack of wood between them on the floor, staring around them.

'I see you've had the decorators in,' one man joked to me, indicating the hall wall, which was in the worst state of repair of any wall in the house. The other man was looking around him in astonishment: at the vast ceilings, the cantilevered wooden staircase and the gaps in the worn hall floorboards. 'Jesus, this is some fucking mental gaff,' he said. 'Do you live here?'

'No,' I said, with reluctance.

Roused from sleep, Patrick appeared at the upstairs banister and called for them to come up. They picked up the planed planks of wood and started to carry them down the hall and up the stairs.

'Mind the chandeliers!' one called out as a piece of wood leaned too close to the bare bulb in the hall.

'Mind the wallpaper! It's just been put up!' the other responded as the far-end piece of the wood struck the flaking wall.

When Kit had come back down again and was reheating our coffee, at some point I wondered aloud what all the wood was for.

'He's building a boat.'

'He's building *what?*' I said, confounded.

'Patrick's building a boat in his room.'

I never knew what Kit was going to come out with next, but the improbable news that a boat-building project was going on in the house, literally over our heads, was so surreal even for him that I could not stop laughing.

'You have got to be kidding me.'

'Come upstairs and look.'

By then, the delivery men had been and gone. The wood was stacked neatly against a wall inside Patrick's room. The hull of a half-built wooden boat occupied the greater part of his floor space. 'I want to sail it to France,' he told me with confidence.

'How will you get it out of the room?' I asked. The boat was already far wider than the door through which the pieces of wood had come. I was utterly abuzz to have actually witnessed a delivery of further makings of this fantastical boat.

'The window,' Patrick said casually, pointing to the enormous eighteenth-century sash window that overlooked the street leading to King's Inns.

I found myself comparing many things in my life with Kit's. We did not, for instance, have an upstairs tenant who was building a boat to sail to France in. Our upstairs neighbour was a taciturn, surly man, whom I found more than once burning pornographic magazines in the back garden on my way to the bike shed. The scorched fragments of these magazines once floated on to our kitchen table on a summer evening when we were eating with the window open while he was incinerating his latest collection in the garden.

The summer I worked in the dole office in my hometown of Ennis, County Clare, mindlessly stamping unemployment dockets, Kit travelled around South America with his then girlfriend, Clara-from-Paris, to visit some of the friends he appeared to have everywhere. I was stuck in an airless office during one of the wettest Irish summers on record, a period when religious statues started to move of their own accord, or so those said who claimed to have witnessed such improbable activity.

When we met after that summer, at the beginning of the new academic year, Kit had something he wanted to show me.

'Shut your eyes,' he instructed.

I shut them.

'Guess what this is,' he said, pouring something gently into my hand. The unseen rough sand that I closed tight into my fist felt like a secret I never wanted to tell him: that I believed I was in love with him, even though we had kissed only once, the first time we had met, walking among the Westmeath meadows when the sun had come up. I opened my eyes to see mysterious black grit in my palm.

'Volcanic ash from Colombia,' Kit said, and I thought it was the most exotic thing I had ever seen in my life.

I was in thrall to these stories from afar, and the Henrietta Street house, and the people Kit attracted to him, from his boat-building classmate upstairs, to the friends who arrived at intervals to stay, from Paris, from London, from Bogotá. I tried to ignore his many girlfriends, who were always coming and going, who I sensed were collectively amused by my earnest, faithful presence in Kit's life, yet I was the one person who remained around longer than all of them.

Milan Kundera's *The Unbearable Lightness of Being* had not long been published, and we were all still reading it: the cult novel with its distinctive Faber and Faber crimson cover was ubiquitous on campus. I had a copy of that edition myself, which I loaned to Kit. He was always interested in what I was reading; literature was the only area of our lives that I felt with confidence I knew more about than he did. When he returned the book, Kit informed me gravely that he had recognized himself in Tomas, the charismatic main character, who feels incapable of fidelity to just one woman.

'I've had a few girlfriends tell me I'm like Tomas,' he said, looking genuinely troubled. 'I think I can see why.'

After he told me he saw himself in Tomas, I carefully reread the novel, using it as a primer, trying to understand Kit better by studying Tomas's character and motivations, although parts of it seemed to speak to me too.

'Love is the longing for the half of us we have lost.'

'He had no idea if it was hysteria or love.'

When not in class, I spent most of my time thinking of Kit and the treasured prospect of our next meeting.

One winter's evening, there was a party at a house on South Frederick Street and everyone in our flat was invited. I had not known there were any domestic houses on South Frederick Street, a Georgian street of offices and the odd café at ground level. The entire house was being rented by another set of architecture students, friends of one of my flatmates. There was a rumour that there was some issue with missing deeds and, in the absence of deeds and the ability to sell on the property, it was in the interim being rented to these architecture students for a tiny rent, in exchange for them taking care of its period features.

This house, I noted, as I went up the stairs, was in a much better state of repair than the one Kit lived in. However, it too was so ferociously cold we could see each other's breath puffing out in front of our faces like empty speech bubbles in a cartoon.

We had been directed at the door to leave coats in the bedroom at the top left of the stairs, the one that overlooked the street. I had my coat under my arm, although I had no intention of taking off the jumper that I was wearing over a dress that had belonged to my mother in the 1960s; I wore most of her vintage clothes through college. It was far too cold to be discarding a jumper for the sake of fashion, even if my fashion was always more than twenty years out of date.

Climbing the stairs, I was already worrying about not being able to talk to anyone and wondering how early I could possibly leave. I functioned reasonably well one on one, or in small groups, but dealing with more than three or four people – and the house was heaving already – made me anxious back then.

I cannot now recall if there were other people in the room with me when I went in to reluctantly deposit my coat. All I remember is what I saw in that room.

A plane. There was a plane in the room. It was more accurate to say that the enormous room was more plane than room, so fully did this plane occupy the space. A bed was in one corner of the room and a rail of clothes in another, but they barely made an impression. The room was pure essence of plane.

I stood inside the door, staring. I registered the wings. The cockpit. The tail. Unlike the boat still under construction at the other side of the Liffey, this plane was complete. Who had built it? How would they get it out of the room? Through the enormous window? But how? Would it ever fly? Where would it go? If the Henrietta Street boat had stirred me, the South Frederick Street plane moved me even more, both as exotic and melancholy as a caged singing bird, trapped within their Georgian rooms.

There were several coats and jackets already stuffed into the cockpit. I stood and stroked one wing of this fantastical plane, already composing the story in my head to deliver to Kit at our next meeting, and how I would make him guess at what it was I had seen in this room; a guess as seemingly impossible as divining Rumpelstiltskin's true name. For once, I would have a story to tell him.

I hung my coat carefully over the plane's left wing, the one closest to the door. It felt as if I was leaving part of myself on a chrysalis, something that would one day metamorphose into flight and go soaring off into the glorious, unknown heights.

Dublin in the 1980s was a city thick with smog. The ban on smoky fuel had not yet come about and, once the winter months arrived, a grey pall hung over everything. I was reading Dickens and felt I now knew what the 'pea-soupers' he kept referring to in *Bleak House* were.

There was both a pea-souper and a sea-fog down on the evening of 2 December 1985, when I cycled across town to UCD. One of my flatmates who attended UCD had tipped me off that Seamus Heaney was to give a reading in the university's Literary and Historical Society, known to all as the L & H. I had never heard him reading before.

The combination of smog and fog made it impossible to see more than a couple of feet ahead. I considered getting off the bike and walking, but I was already a little late and did not want to miss the opportunity to hear this poet that everyone was talking about. I kept going, half expecting to come crashing down at any minute.

The room allocated to the event was too small for the number of people who had turned up. I squeezed into a space near the window, where condensation was steadily trickling down the inside of the pane.

Seamus Heaney arrived. He knew his audience. He told us that the poet Philip Larkin had died earlier that day and, in tribute to him, he was going to read one of his poems. He looked at us mischievously.

'If you remember nothing else about this evening, you'll remember this,' he said, and started to read 'This Be The Verse', while we howled.

'They fuck you up, your mum and dad . . .'

At the end of the reading, Seamus Heaney told us that he had finished a poem just that morning. That he was going to read it to us and that we were to be his very first audience for this poem. The atmosphere in the room quickened. We shifted in our Doc Martens and desert boots. We were collectively proud and excited and thrilled. We were only feckless students who had not yet achieved anything, but a famous poet was going to pay us the honour of reading his new poem to us, a poem literally ink-fresh from his pen. We were going to be a small part of Irish literary history.

The poem Seamus Heaney read to us was 'The Haw Lantern'. 'The wintry haw is burning out of season . . .' it began. The poem was about winter and the Greek philosopher Diogenes, and light and truth. It eventually became the title poem of his next collection, which was published in 1987, the year I finished college. And we were there when he first read that poem, on the day he finished writing it.

That evening, when I cycled back to our Ranelagh flat, the visibility was worse than before. In Dublin Bay, the fog horns sounded their mournful cries again and again. This time, though, I did not see the red lights of bicycle dynamos glowing in front of me. I saw instead the wintry haws of Seamus Heaney's poem, burning out of season.

Midway through my third year, there was a party at Kit's place, and of course I was there. For once, the usual ever-changing girlfriend was not there; she was ill. Kit cooked huge pots of mussels, served up with hunks of bread. There were French cheeses I did not recognize and many bottles of home-made wine someone had brought as a gift. He had bought a bale of briquettes for the fire that evening and it gave out more heat than usual. A tape recording of Vladimir Cosma's soundtrack from Jean-Jacques Beineix's *Diva* was playing at full volume; Kit had introduced me to the 1981 film, a favourite of his, and made a copy of the music for me. I often listened to it on my Walkman while cycling to college; it sounded how I so often felt those days: gothically moody.

Since my last visit, Kit had hung up on the wall his grandfather's familiar tails, white shirt and cravat, now transformed into an eerie two-dimensional presence from the past, as if the dead grandfather were trying to push himself out through the wall. The only light came from the fire and the many lambent candles and tea lights scattered through the room. That night, I thought Kit's room had never looked more atmospheric in its Georgian dereliction.

There were about twenty of us at the party. People smoked joints and kept opening more bottles of wine. I didn't know anyone there except Patrick, and Kit was too busy hosting to spend much time with me. Kit had an inexhaustible number of friends of all ages: I envied his effortless ability for friendship with all kinds of people. I was always uneasily wondering if I belonged in Kit's crowd and, that night, when I found myself too intimidated to start a conversation among these innately confident people, I knew with bitterness that I didn't.

Although I had close friendships with my three flatmates, those had come about because I saw them all the time. I had not made the effort to make many friends at Trinity: none of them seemed to me a quarter as compelling as Kit, the person whom I measured everything by. I had a niggling awareness all along that I was making a grave mistake in not trying to make friends, and the result in my third year, as I was now finding at ad hoc gatherings like this, was that my social skills were close to zero. I had gathered no tools during my university life to construct bridges of conversations with strangers. Was I always, I wondered that night, going to be an observer, rather than a participant?

By the end of the evening, I was still sober and everyone else was either stoned or drunk. Kit was like a happy, affectionate puppy when drunk. He came up to me now and hugged me hard. I hugged him back. I offered to help tidy up and, when I looked around, suddenly everyone had gone, except me.

'Do you want to stay the night?' Kit said, out of drunken nowhere.

My heart started pounding. 'What?'

'You can crash here if you like. It's late. And it's pouring and you'll get soaked on the bike.'

We tumbled in together under the covers of the platform bed he had built. Kit immediately turned over and fell asleep. I lay awake beside him all night, longing for a caress, a kiss, a reaching for me – anything that would acknowledge my tensile waiting presence, all of me afire to finally be so physically close to him in the darkness of night. I even dared to kiss his neck and stroke his back, hoping he would wake up. He did not.

The man who had had so many girlfriends and affairs and had often told me he wondered if he was addicted to sex did not touch me. As the dreadful grey light of morning began to appear, I knew I was finally going to have to accept the inevitable and painful truth: that nothing more than friendship was ever going to happen between myself and Kit, no matter how much I wanted it to.

When Kit woke up, all I wanted to do was get away immediately.

'Do you want coffee?' he asked, yawning, out of bed in one swift movement. I was already out, frantically trying to compose myself. I could feel an unignorable grief rising within me. I did not know how long I would last before I started crying, but I knew I did not want it to start happening in front of Kit.

'No, I'm grand, thanks. I'm going to head off now.'

He heard something in my voice and fixed me with that piercing, questioning gaze. 'You OK?'

'Yeah, I'm fine. Thanks for the party; it was great,' I said, trying to keep a wobble out of my voice. I was definitely going to start crying very soon. 'I've got to get my show on the road now.' I was out the door before he could hug me goodbye, our usual ritual leave-taking of each other.

Things changed after that. I was desperate to claw back some time, some experiences, some friends, some dignity, some anything of college life that was not wholly defined by my futile infatuation with Kit. I avoided Henrietta Street, skipped lectures, tried to write poetry, went exploring the run-down back streets of Dublin and spent a lot of time in O'Neill's, drinking Guinness with the Trinity friends I at last discovered when I awoke from my enthralment.

In my fourth and final year, Kit took a year out. He did not say goodbye and I was not sure where he had gone. One person told me he was in Paris. Another told me he was in Bogotá. I told myself I did not care where he was.

In my last year, I was indeed sometimes maudlin on those afternoons and evenings in the pub, when I thought of Kit and wondered with an ache what he was doing and where he was, but as we were now in our last months of college, most people were even more maudlin when drunk than I. These new friends were mostly melancholy about finishing college and entering a world of work and responsibilities, where we would not go indiscriminately drinking during the day. In the pub, they talked about the best years of our lives coming to an end.

'I know I'm going to really miss college. Will you, Rosita?' I was asked many times.

'Yeah. 'Course I am,' I said vaguely. It was easier to lie. The thought that these four years were the best I was ever going to have filled me with a dread so deep I could not articulate it.

After my final English exam, I ran across Front Square, through Front Arch, out into the noise of College Green, with its green buses trailing exhaust fumes and its sluggish traffic and distracted pedestrians. I was screaming with incoherent joy and uncaring of who was looking at me. I was desperate to leave; to leave Kit behind, to leave university behind, to leave Ireland behind; to slough everything off like a snakeskin and begin again.

A week later, I applied for a year-long working-holiday visa to Australia. I had spent the previous summer working in London to save enough money to buy a ticket to go somewhere after college. Australia was now the furthest place away from Ireland that I could think of. And so that is where I went.

It is many years since I have seen Kit. He lives in France now, in a house in the mountains he designed and built himself, with a woman I have never met and probably never will.

In 2018, a tenement museum opened in a house on Henrietta Street, a few doors down from the house Kit once occupied. 'When you enter 14 Henrietta Street, you'll experience over 300 years of city life in the walls of one address,' reads the home page of its website. 'Our intimate guided tours bring you on a journey from the house's grand Georgian beginnings to the tenement dwellings of its later years. By connecting to the personal stories of those who called 14 Henrietta Street home, the building's hidden histories are revealed.'

It's a very popular visitor attraction, both domestically and internationally. I have never gone. There is no need.

It was a long time before I realized the true value of my friendship with Kit. I had wanted a romantic relationship with him and, in failing to attain it, long considered that our entire friendship had been a catastrophic waste of time. But a brief relationship with Kit would have irrevocably burned the tinder of our friendship right up. We were always so much better as close friends than we would ever have been as lovers and partners. It was he who recognized this, not me, and he who took the care to make sure the deep connection between us was not extinguished by a short fling.

My friendship with Kit was by far the most seminal one of my young adulthood. He made me realize I could tell stories. He instilled in me a longing to travel and see the world. He showed me the richness of what it was to have many friends from many backgrounds and of different ages. But most of all, he gave me the gift of curiosity. In wanting to be like Kit, to have his boundless creativity and curiosity, somewhere along the way, I became a curious person.

THE FRIENDS WHO DIED

In memory of my mother, Catherine, died 19 January 2021

My Mother's Friend

IT WAS A shared love of flowers and gardens that first connected my mother and Elizabeth. They met at their local
Flower Club, in the west of Ireland town I grew up in. Years
ago. Decades ago. In those days, it was an organization frequented exclusively by women.

I was very young when my mother joined the Flower Club.
I never once attended a meeting over all the years of her membership. I don't even know where they met in the town for
these monthly gatherings, except sometimes a room in a local
hotel was rented for a visiting demonstrator and I was aware
that was a particularly well-attended night. Even so, over time,
I became aware of some elements associated with the club.

I became knowledgeable with some of the accoutrements
and language of flower arranging. I did not – and still do not –
automatically think of a pool of drinking water in the desert
when hearing the word 'oasis'. My first introduction to the
word was knowing it to be a block of a green, sponge-like,
gritty-feeling substance. The oasis I knew came in blocks
about the size of half a loaf of bread, which my mother would

then cut down to the size, shape and height she wanted. Then she soaked the oasis in water, water which it retained for days, while maintaining the shape it had been cut into. Sometimes it was a circle, sometimes a rectangle, or a log, or a square. It depended on the shape and size of the flower arrangement for which it was to form the base.

The oasis base weighted with water, she then began a complex process of creating a formal flower arrangement, unbounded by a vase. Some arrangements were meant to be seen in the round, so they had to have blooms visible for the full 360 degrees. Others were to be displayed against walls, so they were constructed to be flattish on one side. Some were for the table, so had to be small and low. I learned a lot about symmetry, just by looking at these flower arrangements.

Sometimes the visiting demonstrators gave a theme in advance and would then judge the Flower Club members' interpretations of these themes. These were high-octane days. I would come home from school to discover the kitchen sink had been commandeered by flowers and greenery, and my mother in the midst of a complicated floral task. The function of the oasis was that you could try out lots of different places to locate particular flowers. Dinner would be left out for my father and myself and then there was a flurry to get ready to be collected to go to the venue, as my mother did not drive.

It was usually Elizabeth who called to collect my mother and her fragile botanical construction. Elizabeth had become my mother's close friend through the club. All my mother's friends were kind to me, but I was always especially pleased to answer the door to Elizabeth. Softly spoken, she was the essence of calmness and dignity. She had dark hair in a cloud and often wore pearls. She was unfailingly elegant in her dress and smelled of a perfume unfamiliar to me but which I came to know as distinctive to her.

'Is Mum ready?' she'd ask, stepping into the hall, bending down to give me a hug.

My mother was usually not ready. She would call from the kitchen that she was just coming, or she'd be brushing her coat down, or making sure my father knew the instructions to prepare whatever it was we were going to eat. While we waited, Elizabeth and I would have short conversations. Their family had a dog, which was the thing I desired most in the world as a child, and I always enviously enquired about this dog. She would ask with genuine interest as to what I was reading and I would tell her.

When my mother finally emerged, I would hold the front door open for the two of them to depart through, and then follow the car up the driveway to close the gates after them. They started talking as soon as they got into the car and, often, my mother was already so absorbed in animated conversation with Elizabeth that she would forget to wave back to me.

The biggest competition event of the year was the County Show in August. This was an agricultural show, where people brought their ponies and calves and dogs; their home-made jams, bread, tarts and cakes; their carrots and potatoes and beans; their roses and dahlias and flower arrangements – all to be judged by judges not from the county, lest there be accusations of nepotism.

In the days preceding the County Show, our bathroom was taken over. Flowers of all colours and scents drifted in the filled bath among sprays of greenery. Years later, when I saw a reproduction of John Everett Millais's painting *Ophelia*, in which Ophelia lies in river water, surrounded by gorgeous flowers, I thought of the bath in our house at County Show time.

On competition day, my mother would get up very early and spend hours working when the flowers were at their freshest. In common with other members of the Flower Club, she entered several categories. They were called things like Best Pedestal Arrangement, Best Use of Colour, Most Original Exhibit, Best Table Arrangement, Best Miniature Arrangement.

On those occasions, my father drove her, with me as helper, to the venue. I was not permitted to carry the arrangements themselves but I was allowed to carry the less precious, albeit essential tools: secateurs, extra oasis, back-up flowers, green wire and a spray-mist bottle of water. She would deposit the arrangements in their allocated categories along the long tables covered with white cloths. Then we would both view the competing entries and I would give them marks out of ten in my head, while my mother congratulated the other women on their arrangements.

I knew perfectly well that no matter what good friends my mother was with Elizabeth and the other women who were members of the Flower Club, and vice versa, when it came to competition time, most of them really, really wanted to win. The acknowledgement of silver cups and red cards (denoting a First Place) mattered. My mother won prizes a lot more often than Elizabeth did, and I always wondered if Elizabeth minded this but of course never dared to ask.

My memories of Elizabeth are impressionistic. They are almost always of me answering the door to her, or of putting my head into the living room to say hello on the days when I came home from school to find the two of them ensconced over the teapot. I don't recall, for instance, ever being in her house, although at Christmas time, I would get out of my father's car and drop off a gift of my mother's home-made baked goods or preserves at their front door.

Along with other members of the Flower Club, they went away several times to London, to the Chelsea Flower Show, and once to visit Monet's Gardens at Giverny in France, an expedition they reminisced about for years. On these occasions, the members teamed up to share hotel rooms, and it was Elizabeth whom my mother always shared a room with. Sometimes they went out locally in Elizabeth's car on outings for lunch together, or they met downtown for morning coffee, or they met up to help out with doing flowers for the local church for some particular occasion.

The two of them just loved to talk. Whenever the phone rang in our house, it was almost always for my mother. My father, a practical man who believed that the telephone was for conversations intended solely for the imparting of some important piece of information, usually completed his calls in under a minute. By contrast, my mother frequently spent hours at a time on the phone, talking to her friends, but especially to Elizabeth.

Our house phone was fancy, an ivory-white contraption, with a shiny raspberry-pink circle of numbers behind the dial. It had a heavy, curved receiver and a flex that inevitably coiled tight; it was my job to periodically untangle this coil. It was the only phone in the house. The phone stood on a ledge in front of a mirror in the hallway and whoever was taking the call usually sat on the bottom of the stairs.

It was partly due to that, and partly out of a desire to offer privacy to the person on the phone, that other household members did not go out into the hall until the call was finished. In the case of the calls between my mother and Elizabeth, this could be a very long time. Sometimes, my need to visit the bathroom was too great to wait any longer and I would tiptoe out past my mother, who remained utterly absorbed in the conversation with her friend.

I grew up, went away to boarding school, then to college. I went travelling. Lived abroad. Had various jobs. Eventually came back and settled in Dublin. Throughout all those years, Elizabeth and my mother stayed close friends. Her husband died. She sold their family home and rented a smaller house. Both of them eventually gave up their membership of the Flower Club, first Elizabeth, and then my mother.

'Elizabeth has moved into a nursing home,' my mother told me when I was visiting one weekend. 'But I think it's temporary. She just needs a rest.'

In the months and years that followed, I drove my mother out to the nursing home on the outskirts of town where Elizabeth had remained, so she could visit. They still talked a lot. By then, they both had mobile phones.

I was away when Elizabeth died in the autumn of 2014. My mother had not known she had had a terminal illness. Recently, she said to me, 'We were such good friends for so many years, but she never told me she was dying.' Of all the many, many things they had confided in each other over the years, this was the one Elizabeth felt unable to tell my mother.

But a couple of days before she died, she asked my mother to do the flowers for her coffin, specifically, white flowers only. My mother, visiting by her bedside at the invitation of family, said yes. When I later heard about this, I felt a pang so profound I thought I would cry. In life, they had bonded over their shared loved of flowers, and now, in death, one had acknowledged the other's long friendship by asking her to create the most meaningful floral arrangement of all. I thought of my octogenarian mother in her kitchen, gallantly snipping stems and stripping leaves and choosing the finest, just-opening blooms; using the skills of a lifetime to honour her newly dead friend as best she could. It nearly broke my heart, to be honest.

My mother is now in her nineties and most of her friends are dead. I don't know what it's like to lose all your peers, one by one, to attend funeral after funeral. If I'm 'lucky', this will someday happen to me too. For me, there are so many opportunities yet to make new friends, while cherishing old friendships I made a long time ago. For my mother, those opportunities to make new friends lessened and lessened over time, as she became older. Then her old friends began to die.

My mother still has my father, and us, her children. There are seven grandchildren and two great-grandchildren. But much as she loves us all, we are family. If you're lucky, as my mother has been, you find friends like Elizabeth with whom you remain close for their entire life, whose friendship sustains you as long as they live, until you have to go on living without them.

My Next-door Neighbour

A few days before Christmas in the winter of the Big Freeze in 2010, I moved into my new house. I had bought it some months previously but was yet to spend a single night there, due to ongoing renovations. In the end, I had to move in, even though the house was still unfinished. It didn't, for instance, have an operating shower at that point. Nor did it have heating, which might not have mattered too much, except for the unfortunate fact that in December that year the temperature was regularly dropping to minus ten and below.

A removal truck had brought my furniture from storage the day before. My focus was now on moving the rest of my personal belongings in. The house, unoccupied and unheated for months, was so cold I could see my breath every time I lugged another box into the kitchen from the car. It started to snow. On one of these trips back and forth from the back gate, the door of the house beside me opened and a man came to our shared back wall.

'I'm Charles,' he said, extending a hand. 'Welcome.'

I stopped my personal courier service to talk to him. Our small terrace of houses had been built in the 1930s, on the site of former allotments that fronted the Georgian houses behind us. Charles had lived in his house all his life; his parents had bought it not long after their marriage. He had grown up and raised his own small family there and now remained there with his wife, Jane. He was a man with many decades behind him, his hair white as the snow that was now falling on us both.

'Will you be using your fire?' Charles enquired, when we had made our short exchange of names and potted histories of our houses; mine, of builders and renovations.

'Definitely.'

When I came out of the house later that day, after depositing boxes in different rooms, I discovered an offering of fuel at my back door. There was a bale of briquettes, a bag of coal and a bag of sticks. There was even a box of matches. I stared at it in amazement. I had had the chimney cleaned during the renovations, but in the flurry to move in and get everything out of the storage warehouse where it had been on an expensive holiday in a different part of Dublin, buying fuel had not even occurred to me. There had been no time and no head space. The short December day was now getting dark and even colder, but suddenly, miraculously, I had the makings of a fire in my house that still did not have heating.

'I hope you don't mind me leaving that there for you.' It was Charles again, in a jacket this time, a little tentative.

'This is from you?'

'We don't light our own fire very often any more,' he said. 'Our fuel is stored in there.' He indicated the wooden shed in his garden that was also a garage.

That evening, I lit a volcanic fire with my donated fuel. I slept on the couch in front of the fire, waking up now and then to see the embers glowing, warm in the pocket of heat the fire cast in the otherwise sub-zero room.

The house I had bought is, as a friend once described it, a house with two fronts. The actual front looks on to a busy, narrow avenue and is part of a long stretch of houses of different periods. The back looks on to a cul de sac, which has a different name to the avenue, a lovely ad hoc horseshoe of some sixteen houses.

I got to know the rest of my neighbours gradually. A man whose name I didn't even know yet that December saw me struggling one morning to get my car out from the compacted snow and ice it was frozen into. He disappeared into his house and came back with a bucket of ashes, which gave the tyres enough traction for a grip. Four others came together one afternoon to share tools and labour to attach a bolt to my back wall to lock my bike to.

All that winter, I regularly came home from work to discover logs or briquettes or coal at my back door, left there by my next-door neighbour. I didn't have to buy fuel once that winter. It was the ultimate housewarming gift, if you like. I offered to pay for it, but Charles just laughed and said he was glad the house next door wasn't empty any more.

After that Christmas, we had hundreds of short chats at our shared back wall and at our front doors. I learned a lot about cricket; he was a long-standing member of the local club and knew every national and international score. He had a key for the door to the club in the street wall near us and went there at some point every day to socialize. In the spring, I gave him purple lilac from my back garden, and in the summer, he gave me yellow roses from his front garden. I sometimes came home to find he had mowed my lawn for me. We exchanged gifts at Christmas. I still keep my very favourite decorations in a seasonal reindeer tin he gave me that came with biscuits in it.

Charles was the perfect neighbour, kind, thoughtful and never intrusive. He always had the news on everyone in our neighbourhood and yet he was never a gossip, which is a truly rare combination. He was a genuinely good man, whom I never heard say anything unkind about anyone. The most he ever did to express a less than tolerant opinion was to occasionally roll his eyes when imparting some piece of news.

Whenever my visiting family or friends got locked out, as they did more often than you might think, they went next door to get the keys and always ended up being invited in for tea. On summer evenings, when I was sitting out the back with friends, he'd always wave when he was coming in from the garage and, no matter what stage of the hosting I was at, I'd always go over to say hello and catch up.

When Jane fell ill some years ago, he was selfless in caring for her at home. When she died in 2016, I was out of the country. I arranged to send flowers and hesitated on the Inter-flora website for some time over what to write on the accompanying card. 'From your friend and neighbour,' I wrote eventually, surprising myself at the truth of describing myself as his friend. Before I wrote the message for the card, I had not realized, or understood, that friendship could be created from such small fragments of regular interaction over time. Our conversations over the years had been many, but most were probably no longer than five minutes. We never once sat down for a meal together.

The last time I saw my next-door neighbour, he was, typic-ally, looking out for me. I had come back from an overnight reporting assignment out of Dublin and he told me an inter-loper had been parking in my space while I had been away. The biggest sin one can commit in our little cul de sac is to park in someone else's space.

'I was keeping an eye out for the fella, so I could tell him off, but I missed him,' Charles said. 'But I got the registration number.'

I told him where I had been away working and what I had been doing. He mentioned how well his red geraniums were still doing, despite the winter chill, and I duly looked over the wall and admired them. It began to rain and we said our good-byes and made for our respective back doors.

A few days later, I had a call at work in the morning from another neighbour with the news. Charles had died suddenly. He had been found in a state of collapse by his son the previ-ous morning, who had come to collect him for an outing, and had died later in hospital the same day.

I was stunned. I got up from my desk and stood in the cor-ridor outside our communal kitchen, the phone still clamped to my ear, even when the call had ended, trying to compre-hend what had been said to me. It just could not be true. Then a text came in from his son, to tell me himself.

At his funeral on a bitterly cold November morning, the Leinster Cricket Club, of which Charles had been a member for a remarkable seventy-six years, made a guard of honour for him on the steps of the local church. His neighbours were among the assembled congregation and, as his coffin was carried up the church steps, I found myself unexpectedly inconsolable.

Those dozens of small kindnesses over the years and our many short conversations had, unbeknownst to me, incremen-tally added up over time to a significant depth of feeling. The upshot was that I was absolutely undone on the day of Charles's funeral by the knowledge I would never again see my friend and next-door neighbour. I went to the burial and then to the funeral lunch, and then I went home and wept some more at the realization I had seen his white head at our shared back wall for the last time.

My fire is lighting as I write this. The fuel Charles gave me is long since burned. But I have not forgotten him, nor the fact that the very first fire I lit in my house was made from fuel given to me by the next-door neighbour who became such a dear friend. A chain of light and heat and kindness began that December night that warms my house still, and always will.

My Friend's Friend

I met my friend Anna when I was looking for a house share in Dublin, ages ago. In the last century. A mutual friend had told me that there was a house on Upper Leeson Street where a room was going for rent. One girl had just moved out, to live with her boyfriend, and the remaining three were seeking a new housemate. A phone call was made, via a landline, and a viewing-slash-interview visit organized.

At the kitchen of the Leeson Street house, I was given a mug of tea and thoroughly grilled by the assembled three.

'Have you ever shared a house before?' This was Monica. I wondered if she was joking. Didn't everyone share accommodation in their student and post-student days? It was only later I realized that she was wondering if I was house-trained: would I be amenable to a cleaning rota and other important elements of making a shared house pleasant for all, or was I instead a muck savage to be avoided, who did not know how to pick up after herself?

'We change rooms every six months, because some are bigger than others. Would you mind that?' asked Liz. There were four bedrooms of varying sizes. One room in the house was so large we called it Croke Park, after Ireland's giant sports stadium. Croke Park came with two huge windows overlooking Leeson Street and its own en suite. The smallest room, by contrast, was narrow as a barge, a room we called the Boat. Other house shares thought we were mad to be disrupting ourselves every six months, but it worked for us.

'Where are you from?' Anna asked. She, it emerged, was from a town in County Galway. And then she told some story. I can't even remember which one it was, except it was funny and irreverent and, from the way she told it, I suspected there were many more from whence that one had come.

I passed the test and subsequently lived in the Leeson Street house with the Leeson Street Ladies, as we called ourselves, for about two and a half years. Our various friends and boyfriends were always coming and going from the Leeson Street house. One of them was Anna's long-time friend from school, Sadhbh.

Sadhbh lived in Barcelona and worked teaching English as a foreign language. She would arrive periodically from Spain while en route to visit her family in County Mayo. Sadhbh would more or less tumble in the door, talking before she even crossed the threshold, dumping her chaotic belongings in the hall. She addressed us individually as 'babe'. Collectively, we were 'chicas'.

'Babe, I'm dying for a cigarette; have you got a match? I lost my lighter.' Sadhbh was always losing things. Her glasses, for instance. My then boyfriend once found her passport and a bundle of cash which had fallen down behind a cabinet in the living room, where she had been sleeping on the couch. The six of us had spent hours searching for the passport. She had not even noticed the money was missing.

'Babe, let's open the Rioja now. It's a good one.' Sadhbh knew all the best years for Spanish wines, which Reserva was the one to drink, which vineyard was the best.

'Babe, I brought my cards with me.' Sadhbh read Tarot cards, a fact which both fascinated and terrified me. I did not want my cards read.

She would sit down at our round kitchen table with a mug of tea or a tumbler of wine, push her glasses back, run her fingers through her spiky hair, then launch into stories about her Barcelona life. Sadhbh, along with her teaching job, co-presented a weekly show called *Radio English Teacher*, which, from the way she told it, sounded like an audio version of *Fawlty Towers*. Listeners were inadvertently cut off mid-call, there was unscheduled on-air swearing, there was hungover ad-libbing.

Sadhbh was Anna's friend, and I hadn't known Anna her-self long then, but I sometimes went out with them when Sadhbh was visiting; out to our local pubs, O'Brien's or the Lee-son Lounge. Sadhbh usually talked at top speed. Listening to the two of them reminisce and playfully slag each other off and swap stories was like witnessing verbal jazz. I mostly listened on these occasions, both a little dazzled and envious at the ease with which they conversed. This friendship went way back, back to their teenage years and a shared past history I could only guess at. I did not have a single friend from my schooldays.

I still have a postcard Sadhbh sent to 'Anna and Co.' at our Leeson Street house, after one of her visits. It's dated 11 Feb-ruary 1998, a reproduction of a painting of a woman tinged with yellow, her gaze downwards. It's written in untidy bright blue pen, thanking us for hosting her before Christmas. She writes: 'I may even see you here on holliers betimes?' And ends with, 'Anyway, chicas, love and respect, Sadhbh,' fol-lowed by a string of kisses.

Early the following summer, Anna and I did indeed go out to Barcelona to visit Sadhbh. I was not feeling very sociable. I had recently broken up with the man I believed I would marry and I was not processing it at all well. I spent part of the time by myself, writing my diary in cafés and bars and mindlessly wandering around the streets and shops of the Ramblas, some-times crying as I wandered. I tried to be chipper when the three of us met up for meals. I did not want to dump yet more break-up angst on Anna, who had – like all my friends back then – heard more than they ever needed to about my sun-dered relationship.

It was Anna who asked me how I thought Sadhbh was. I was so self-absorbed with my heartbreak I had hardly noticed.

We had gone with her to the studio as special guests of a recording of *Radio English Teacher*, and it had been as funny and entertaining and slap-dash as she had described. She had brought us to beautiful restaurants, where people ate fantastically late. She had given us a list of places she thought we should see, and they had all been very worth seeing, in so far as I could gauge through the general fog that encompassed me at the time.

'How do you think Sadhbh is? I'm kind of worried about her.'

'Is she not OK?' I said. I didn't want to have this conversation. I was not OK myself. I did not think I was able to make the effort to be concerned about anyone else.

Anna did not think Sadhbh was OK. She was worried about various aspects of her behaviour, which she pointed out to me. She was worried about certain things Sadhbh said and did in public. She was worried she was smoking too much weed. I had assumed this was all part of Sadhbh's *œuvre*; her large and vocal personality; the way she chose to live her life. But Anna, who knew her long-time friend intimately, knew that this was in some way out of the ordinary. Knew that this was not OK.

That evening, we went to meet Sadhbh in her apartment, before going for dinner. We had not been in her apartment before. All the shutters were down, although it was not yet evening. I was disconcerted by the dimness. We waited for Sadhbh to get ready.

'Come on in, chicas,' she called to us from her room.

Sadhbh's bedroom was spartan. The only thing in it was a mattress on the floor and, beside it, a sizable pile of pistachio shells. All I could think of when I looked at the pile of shells was an animal, an animal's lair. I didn't know why they were on the floor, why Sadhbh hadn't picked them up. They looked like they had been there a long time. They disturbed me.

Less than a week after our sojourn in Barcelona, when we were back in Dublin, Anna received an unexpected call from Sadhbh's brother.

'Liam is going over to Barcelona. To bring Sadhbh home,' she told me. 'She's not well.'

'What's wrong with her?'

Anna was pacing the kitchen, biting her nails, something she never did. 'She's having some kind of breakdown. He told me he was going to pack up her apartment for her. He was kind of vague about it all. But he's bringing her home.'

In the days that followed, there were many phone calls between Anna and Sadhbh's family. She was now at home in Belmullet, staying with her parents, resting. Liam had indeed brought her home from Spain, along with all her belongings. I found it difficult to believe Anna and I had been walking around Barcelona with Sadhbh so very recently, with her pointing out landmarks to us of the city she knew so well, when she was now so suddenly and completely gone from her life there and living back in Mayo.

About a week later, I turned on the radio to listen to the seven o'clock news while I was getting up. There was a report of a woman missing in Mayo. Liz was in the kitchen making breakfast when I went downstairs.

'There's something on the news about a woman gone missing,' I said vaguely, buttering toast and making coffee.

Liz was in a hurry. She picked up her bag and ran out the door. 'See you later!' she called back to me.

That afternoon in the office, my landline phone rang. This was years before mobiles. It was Liz. She never called me at work. I had never called her either. I didn't even know what her work number was.

'Rosita,' she said. Liz sounded weird, I thought distractedly. I wondered why she was calling. Was I to get something for dinner on the way home? Were there plans to go out? Had my former boyfriend possibly called her with a message for me?

'Remember what you told me this morning?'

I couldn't. I was having trouble concentrating back then, lost as I was in a grief that seemed unending. 'No,' I said.

'That woman who was missing. The thing you heard on the news.'

I stared down at my keyboard. It was filthy. It needed to have all the keys taken off and the accumulation of crumbs and dust cleaned out.

'That was Sadhbh. She went for a walk and didn't come back.'

It couldn't be Sadhbh. It must be someone else, I thought.

'Her brother rang Anna. There are people out looking for her now.'

'But we saw her in Barcelona only a fortnight ago,' I said. In my mind, Sadhbh was still in Barcelona, still searching for her perpetually lost lighter, still talking non-stop.

'It's definitely Sadhbh,' Liz said.

Sadhbh had gone for a drive with her parents to Black Sod the previous evening. Black Sod was right down the bottom of the Mullet peninsula, itself an extremely remote place. It was June and the evenings were long and bright. They had gone for a walk and then split up. A time was arranged to meet back at the car. Sadhbh did not arrive at the appointed time.

Anna, distraught, confounded, shocked, went to Belmullet to be with Sadhbh's family. I lay in bed all that night, unable to sleep. It seemed such a travesty to be in a warm bed when we didn't know where Sadhbh was, except it was virtually certain she herself was not in a bed that night. I told myself she might be just lying low in a shed somewhere, at the end of someone's garden, taking time out for a while. The guards had asked people to check the outbuildings on their land. Nothing was found.

It soon seemed inevitable that Sadhbh had somehow gone into the ocean. There was only the one road leading out of the peninsula and nobody had seen her on it. By then, back in Dublin in the Leeson Street house, Monica, Liz and I all slowly realized that what people were looking for in Mayo was a body.

For days, Sadhbh's family and teams of volunteers walked the beaches twice a day up and down the coastline after high tide. 'She didn't come back on the first tide,' Anna told me on the phone. 'So we are still looking, but we're really waiting for the ninth day.' On the ninth day of a body being lost at sea, gases are released that make it temporarily buoyant. It's usually the last chance a body has of being washed into shore, before it sinks for ever. It's why the families of fishermen who become lost congregate day after heartbreaking day on the piers and shores close to where the drowned person last departed.

Sadhbh came ashore on the ninth day, some distance up the Mullet peninsula from where she had last been seen. Gifted back to her family from the ocean and horizon into which she had disappeared, she was wearing a ring Anna had given her years before.

Liz, Monica and I drove up together in the one car for the removal and funeral. We stopped somewhere along that long journey west to buy flowers. I went in and chose white lilies.

'From your friends in Leeson Street,' I wrote on the card along-side our names, disbelieving the fact that Sadhbh would never again explode through our door like a whirling dervish, incanting 'babe' and 'chicas' to us. I don't even know why I chose lilies. I hate them. They smell of death.

On the morning of the funeral, Anna, very pale and very composed, finished writing the eulogy over breakfast in the Belmullet guest house we were all staying in. The family had asked her to do it, in tribute to their long and close friendship. I watched Anna at her terrible task with a kind of awe, as she wrote and edited stories about the attributes of her friend of a lifetime. Those stories from school and college and the journey into adult life, stories they told and retold to each other, which I had listened in to on our madcap nights together in the Leeson Street pubs: who could ever have guessed that one of these two friends would so soon be incanting the story of the other's life at their funeral?

In the church at Carne, Anna stood at the lectern and read her piece with both calmness and urgency. The eulogy that had been finished hardly an hour before began with a meditation on friendship.

'Over the past week and a half, I've thought a lot about the meaning of friendship, how important it is and how powerful and influential a good friend can be,' she began.

'When I first got to know Sadhbh we were both teenagers, and from then on we were always in and out of each other's lives – coming and going, emigrating and returning – always a constant presence. Gradually, over the years, our lives and identities became intertwined, so much so that when I heard the news last week I stopped and looked around my house and my life and realized how much she had left of herself, physically and spiritually. Her clothes are hanging in my wardrobe. All of her postcards, tapes, books, memories.

'But I was not the only one thinking like this. For many people sitting here today, Sadhbh is, and was, one of the constant underlying themes in their life. She left bits of herself wherever she went, small, carefully chosen pieces of herself. Postcards crammed with anecdotes and observations, letters written on the backs of menus, quotations, philosophy, poetry.'

I still have Anna's eulogy. I kept a copy. After the funeral, I thought a lot about horizons, places defined by being perpetually distant and thus unknowable, both as real at a distance and insubstantial close up in their way as rainbows. I thought about Sadhbh being out in the Atlantic for all those days, drifting among the fish and being turned by the waves, all the while still wearing Anna's ring. She was both in and out of the world, in the water and far from land, while people who loved her walked the liminal area of where she had last been seen and tried so hard to find her, to reel her back in.

Sadhbh was only thirty-one when she died, more than two decades ago. For many of us at that funeral, she was the first of our peers to die. Anna and I have since become close friends ourselves. We have been through more bereavements; through heartbreaks and joys; through career triumphs and personal triumphs; through some very difficult times when we have turned to each other in need of kindness and trusted advice. I'm not sure about many things, but I am sure that Anna is a friend for life. Someone I know recently remarked that a close friend is the one whose call you will always take when you see their name come up, no matter what you're doing. Even if just to say you can't talk now but will call them back very soon. Anna has long been one of those friends.

I never even thought about it until now, but Anna and I have been friends longer than she and Sadhbh were. Something feels wrong about that metric to me. Improbable, perhaps, rather than wrong. Improbable and unlikely. Yet it's true.

I'm so sad for Anna that she lost all that shared history when Sadhbh went into the horizon, that vital anchor to her past. We can always make new friends, but the newer our friends, inevitably, the more it is about our shared futures instead of also our pasts. It's truly a rare thing to have a close friend who has been in your life all your formative years and beyond. That's the one friendship you can never make in later life. It's a friendship rooted in the years when you are both teenagers, trying to figure out the world together, still trying to discover the people you will each become. In years to come, Sadhbh and Anna should have grown old reminiscing about those stories and all the new ones they would have created together ever since, over the last two decades.

Not long ago, Anna told me she had come across a cassette tape of one of Sadhbh's *Radio English Teacher* shows, the one we were guests on, that time long ago in Barcelona. She hasn't listened to it yet. Someday, we'll listen to it together and hear Sadhbh's voice again, a voice which I have now forgotten. I'm hoping very much she'll say 'babe' or 'chicas' on the tape and bring us back to that brief intersection of time when the three of us were all still young and all still in the same world together.

SOUVENIR FRIENDS

THE ULTIMATE SOUVENIR from travelling elsewhere in the world is a friend.

There are, of course, the memories of the experience itself. Those are stored in my head, and another version is contained in the diaries I keep on every journey. There are the few small material souvenirs that had to fit into a pocket in my rucksack and be carried onwards for months. A silver beaker from Tibet that I bought in an antique shop in northern Pakistan. A century-old printed Persian cloth, bought in Isfahan. A tiny packet of gold leaf from a temple in Myanmar. A small brightly coloured painting from a market in Ecuador. A spice box from India that still retains a smell of the long-vanished spices it once contained.

I love and treasure these beautiful little objects. Because I was always travelling so light, I restricted myself to finding one (if even one) portable thing from each country I visited. They are scattered throughout my house now, tiny touchstones to adventures in other cultures, journeys made years ago but which never really ended.

In the course of those travels, I met so many people of all ages. So many shared experiences. So many dinners together, or drinks in bars. So many long train or bus rides. Days spent trekking. Going out exploring cities. Romantic flings, where any schedule was temporarily abandoned in favour of spending more time with each other. Telling and hearing so many stories.

I look back in my diaries and, although I recall many of these experiences vividly, often, the memories of the people with whom I shared them have faded away. We met briefly, had wondrous times and moved on; on to the next train, the next bus, the next stage of our various journeys. I loved those shared times: expendable as fireworks; glorious while they lasted but ephemeral by nature.

And I also love the friends still in my life whom I first met out on the road: my souvenir friends.

Nancy

I met Nancy in a hostel in Kraków during the Easter of 1993. Or rather, I heard her before I saw her. She arrived late off a train from Budapest, when the hostel was already dark for the night. I heard swearing in an Irish accent – 'Bollocks!', followed by a giggle – and 'Whoops!' as she banged into a bunk bed in the dark. The people not yet asleep in the dormitory, including me, giggled also.

The next morning, on my way to the bathroom, I noticed with surprise a copy of Derek Walcott's *Omeros* on the opposite bunk.

'Who's travelling with poetry?' I asked of the dormitory in general, lifting the book up like a detective brandishing an important clue. In my experience, backpackers did not usually travel with books of poetry.

'Me,' said the girl with the Irish accent, who had just come back from the bathroom. It was Nancy. Within a few minutes, we discovered that we had some acquaintances in common, via Trinity, where we had both studied English, Nancy six years after me.

'Will we go and have breakfast?' one of us suggested.

It was not long after 10 a.m. by the time Nancy and I found a café on the main square in Kraków's Old Town. Easter Sunday bells were ringing, women were carrying yellow flowers upside down and there were stalls with painted eggs. We ordered breakfast and stayed there, talking and ordering more coffees, and then, as midday came and went, glasses of wine. We could not stop talking. Nancy had just finished college and was living in Budapest for a year, teaching literature. She had taken the train to Kraków for her Easter holiday. I was four months into an open-ended backpacking trip around Greece, Italy, Eastern Europe and Turkey.

We traded stories like chess masters playing games. Every time one story ended, another began. We each had an endless supply, and we each realized almost at once that day that we were always going to be friends. The one mystery was how we had never met each other before. Twice, different dour-faced women came over to our table to ask us to stop laughing. To stop laughing! This only made us laugh harder.

The café closed at 3 p.m., so we left in search of a bar. We found one, and then, a few hours later, a restaurant. When that closed, we bought beers and went back to the hostel and kept talking. When the dormitory settled down to sleep for the night, we locked ourselves into a bathroom and kept talking. We talked for sixteen hours straight that first day. At the end of it, we declared our love for each other.

Until I met Nancy, I hadn't realized one could truly love a friend; I had assumed such love was only for those men I fell in love with and had sexual relationships with. It's not true. Of course we can love the friends we have platonic relationships with too, which is why it hurts so much when sometimes they break up with us.

A few months after we met, when Nancy had finished out her academic year's teaching and I was still travelling, we arranged to meet in Istanbul and do some travelling together. Nancy had a guidebook to Turkey and was fixated on a photograph that had been taken somewhere far in the east, in the Kaçkar Mountains, close to the border with Armenia.

'I want to go there,' she said simply. 'It looks so beautiful.'

The photograph was of a delicate stone bridge arched like a bracelet over a fervently rushing river. There were mountains in the background. The place was a village called Ayder.

So, on the lure of this one image, we got on a succession of buses and headed east. The journey took four days. We stayed for two weeks in Ayder's only hotel, a modest wooden structure called Otel Caglayan, the Waterfall Hotel, named after one of the many cataracts that tumbled down the verdant mountains. The entire region was spectacularly gorgeous and lush; rare flowers bloomed and botanists visited from all over the world. The road ended at Ayder. It was a summer village; in the winter there was so much snow the place was cut off and everyone moved down to Çamlıhemşin. One local man had stayed the previous winter, living in the thermal bathhouse, the hammam, braving 'wolves and bears and things like that' to trek down to Çamlıhemşin to buy tobacco.

We heard all this from Turkish friends we made in the local cafés, where we went every day to write letters and in our diaries. Both Nancy and I wanted to be writers and we practised by telling stories, tossing out subjects to each other in a manner we named 'story jukebox' and then weaving these words into true stories from our lives. Each day, she told me more about her life: about the big house in Dublin belonging to the grandmother and bachelor uncle she had gone to live with as a small child when her parents divorced.

Years later, Nancy wrote a brilliant and unconventional memoir about this house, where she now lived permanently; about her family and the sheep farm she and her husband took on as part of the estate. When I first read her book, I thought not of the County Dublin house and farm where it was set but of the Turkish Kaçkar Mountains we could see out of the windows of our little hotel as, day after day, Nancy compellingly told me about these people she would one day write about.

One of the friends we had made, Ozan, who ran our hotel, wrote poetry. When he heard that I, too, sometimes wrote poetry, he asked me to help him translate a couple of his poems into English. They were love poems to the girl he hoped to marry. They were very good. The three of us sat for hours in cafés, talking. Ozan was also a mountain guide. He knew every path and track. He had seen wolves. And bears. And things like that.

The women of the village wore chiffon scarves of different colours, edged with beading as beautiful as jewellery. Twisted over them, they added silk scarves from Iran, knotted in rich tangles of colour. Both Nancy and I coveted our own chiffon scarves. Ozan told us there were women in Çamlıhemşin who made them. We took a dolmus down there and both put in an order, returning three days later to collect them. Nancy's was in blue chiffon, decorated with pearls, which made her – as she said with delight – look like a sexy Virgin Mary. Mine was more *French Lieutenant's Woman*: black chiffon edged with emerald-green glass beads. We put them on immediately.

Nancy and I went to the hammam most days, a small building on the edge of the village. We either had a key, or it was unlocked. I can't recall. We certainly never paid to use it. It was here the man had wintered out the previous year and kept warm. We kept our swimsuits on, just in case someone walked in.

'Look,' Nancy said one afternoon as she sat down into the thermal bath. 'What's that?' And she pointed to something small and shiny in the water near us. We examined the little conical silver piece of metal.

'It's a bullet!' she said. We had both seen bullet holes in the past, but neither of us had ever seen a bullet before. We were thrilled and bewildered, but mostly thrilled. We were already concocting a story as to how it might have got there.

When we met Ozan next, Nancy showed it to him and asked, 'Ozan, do you know why was there a bullet at the bottom of the hammam pool?'

Ozan was entirely unfazed by this astonishing question. 'There are many secrets in Ayder,' was all he would say, mysteriously.

It's on my mantelpiece now, still the only bullet I've ever seen. Those two weeks in Ayder, a place both Nancy and I would be afraid to go back to, so perfect was it and so absolutely undeveloped, were defined by the mists that descended each afternoon. It was a kind of enchanted, utterly beguiling place, a place I have never again found anywhere like. I wrote in my diary in late June:

Most days, for half of every day, the clouds settle in the valley and the landscape disappears from sight. All of yesterday, the landscape melted into the damp air. I wrote letters at the kitchen table of the Otel Caglayan and tried to define this place, over and over again. I wrote that I felt at home in a landscape that went into hiding and a damp mist that beaded every strand of uncovered hair. I wrote of writing a page of a story that I left out on the upstairs balcony and how, when I remembered it hours later, the mist had rendered the words indecipherable. Of Ayder being the coolest and dampest place in all of Turkey, with hues of green I had never seen before.

Along with telling stories, one of our things was writing long letters to each other. A couple of years after Nancy and I met in Poland, I went on a long trip to Asia. Those were the days before the internet. I carried guidebooks, traveller's cheques, my diary and a stash of my favourite writing paper, something called onion-skin paper, which had a pleasing crinkle in its near-weightless sheets.

Among the most special joys of that journey were the periodic trips I made to American Express offices to collect my mail. At that time, there were two options to receive post overseas: either through a post office's poste restante service or at the local AmEx office. I used AmEx, because they held letters longer, which was useful, as I was never certain where I was going to be, or when.

The record number of letters in one cache on that journey was eighteen. I picked it up in Agra; it included one from Nancy. I savoured those precious letters for an entire day, reading them in a rooftop café overlooking the Taj Mahal.

I had hopes of exceeding this haul that Christmas. My drop for December was at Panaji, in Goa. My plan was to save them and read them on Christmas Day. But when I arrived at the local AmEx office, there was only one measly postcard, from a fellow traveller I had met in India. From my regular correspondents, there was nothing. Zero. Nada. I eventually discovered there was some kind of strike at a sorting hub in Europe. None of those letters sent that month ever reached me.

It was two months before I got to my next mail drop, in Delhi. Among the letters awaiting me was one from Nancy, who was then studying at Oxford. Nancy wondered why I hadn't mentioned her Christmas gift in the letter I had sent after December. Along with the letter that had never arrived, neither had the gift. And what a gift.

I was reading my letters in a café in Connaught Place in Delhi. When I read what Nancy had posted to me from Oxford, thousands of miles away, I laughed so hard that people turned to stare. I could not stop. I thought someone would come over to chide me, as those people had when Nancy and I had first met and were howling with kinship and merriment in the Kraków café on that Easter Sunday.

I sent you a side of smoked salmon in case you were homesick, Nancy had written. *I was going to send brown bread and a lemon, too, but I thought they might go off.*

You can only celebrate a friend who considers it impractical to post a lemon and brown bread to India from England but who believes it is perfectly fine to send a side of smoked salmon – a flying fish, if you like – on the same hopeful journey.

My last mail drop on that journey was about two months later, in Istanbul. Unsurprisingly, American Express did not operate in Iran, which I travelled through on my way back to Turkey. In my bundle was a fat envelope from Nancy. The envelope emanated a peculiar smell, which got stronger when I opened it up. In her letter, Nancy wrote:

> This morning, I woke to a loud knock on the door. The postman had a large package wrapped in a plastic bag for me. He had it at arm's length. 'It smells a bit unusual,' he said, passing the pen for me to sign. 'Do you know what's in it?'
>
> One look at its smeared address and familiar scrawl was enough for me. 'Yes,' said I. 'Smoked salmon.'
>
> The postman was impressed. 'It seems,' he said, in a tone reminiscent of Sherlock Holmes, 'to have been to India.'
>
> 'Yes, yes,' said I faintly. 'I sent it there myself.'
>
> 'Ahh,' said the postman. 'I think it has passed its sell-by date.'

I laughed so much I actually cried. Nancy had done some heroic work on attacking the stinking parcel, so determined was she to retrieve the thirteen-page letter she had written to me for Christmas. That was what was smelling: the pages infused with the unmistakable smell of rotten fish. She had pegged the pages of the letter on to the clothes line to air, and then sent them out again, this time to Istanbul. I still have all her letters. And that Christmas letter, even so many years later, still retains a hint of the smoked salmon it once accompanied to India. And back.

That first day we met, during our epic talking and story-telling marathon, Nancy ordered a dessert in the Kraków restaurant we were in. She had consulted her little Polish dictionary while ordering.

'It's got gold in it,' she announced delightedly.

'I'm having one too.'

A dessert involving gold seemed fantastically exotic to us both, as exotic as the day had been; the experience of finding so whole and complete a friend, where we already felt we had known each other for ever.

Our 'desserts' arrived. They were two small glasses of clear liquid. We wondered if they were meant to be served on a golden plate, or if the order had got mixed up. High as kites on wine and stories, we craved this fairy-tale gold dessert, part of the fabulous narrative of our Easter Sunday together in Poland that we would keep retelling each other in the future.

Nancy called the waitress over. She returned with a bottle of the clear liquid and held it out between us. We both stared blankly at it.

'Złoto?' Nancy said, referring back to the menu; the Polish word for gold. We were treasure seekers on a quest. We were in our twenties, with our whole lives before us. Nancy was travelling with poetry and I was travelling with my diary and gold was required to transmute this already magical day into something even more valuable. We were then, as we always are, seeking out the most ridiculously romantic version of things.

The waitress suddenly took the bottle back and, with one swift movement, turned it upside down. Gold flakes started drifting down through the vodka within. The bottle was illuminated against the light, and it seemed alive, a kind of golden snow globe. Shimmering and glowing and glimmering in the light, the bottle was lifted and suspended over our heads, as beautiful as some artefact unearthed unexpectedly from a museum's vaults.

I can see it still, the glinting fragments pulsing and turning in the clear liquid, that ever-moving golden thing our friendship of three decades has turned out to be.

India

I met India in India, two years after I met Nancy. We first ran into each other briefly in the fort town of Jaisalmer, in Rajasthan, where the thing to do was go on dubiously run camel treks for several days into the surrounding desert. There is always a backpacker trail in any country, of the unmissable places to go.

Despite the vast size of India, I frequently ran into fellow backpackers more than once by chance. Or, if you wanted to see each other again and had even the vaguest idea about when you might be where, you made arrangements, such as being at a certain place for noon on a certain day, in the hope they might turn up. Or you went to a guest house the two of you had picked out of the guidebook as a place you might stay and left messages for each other at the reception there.

I see from my diary of that time that I had arranged with two new Scottish friends I'd met back in Delhi to be by the chai stalls at the main gate in Jaisalmer on a particular day. I was wearing an ankle-length shot-silk emerald-green dress I had recently got made in Goa, which had medieval-type sleeves that hung in a V. I loved that ridiculous dress so much, which looked even more ridiculous with my rucksack over it, but I didn't care. My new Scottish friends did not turn up but, as I waited, I saw an Australian man whom I had met at a guest house in Bombay – now Mumbai – a couple of months previously.

'Paul!' I called to him. He was entirely unsurprised to see me.

'Hi, Rosita!' he said. He was with an English girl about my age. 'This is India. Do you want to come to lunch with us?'

The three of us went for lunch together, another ad hoc

lunch, as I thought at the time, with someone I'd never met before and probably never would again; India was leaving for Delhi on an afternoon bus.

Except India and I ran into each other again, back in Delhi. She moved into my Par Ganj guest house, which was deemed to be nicer than hers. We went to the markets together and had dinner together in places where beer arrived in tea-pots, so as not to offend the Hindu people in the restaurant. She was a photographer whose photographer boyfriend was coming to India on a newspaper assignment at some point soon, although she was unsure when. We were waiting for Paul to show up, as arranged, but he never did, in the merry-go-round way we all had back then of getting on and off the backpacking carousel whenever we liked.

Holi was coming up, the ancient Hindu festival which means spring is coming and signifies a new beginning when inhibitions are released as people start afresh. More prosaic-ally, it is also the time when excitable young men take the opportunity to chase after women of all ages and pelt them enthusiastically with coloured powder and water.

'I don't want to be in Delhi for Holi,' India said over break-fast the day we had given up on Paul joining us.

'Me neither.'

'Will we go to Manali?'

Manali was a mountain village in Himachal Pradesh, a sixteen-hour bus journey north of Delhi. I had recently managed to get my Iranian visa, a country I was planning to travel through after Pakistan. My most recent plan was to travel north-west to Amritsar from Delhi and then cross the border from there into Pakistan. But what were plans for, except to be remade? India's company was great fun. I could go to Pakistan later.

'Sure!' I said.

Two days later, we left our guest house by cycle rickshaw on our way to the bus station. We had each taken dozens of rickshaws during the course of our travels. We sat in the back seat together, our rucksacks strapped on, chattering away. It was early morning but, even so, the streets were a mass of other rickshaws, Ambassador cars, food hawkers, cows, pedestrians and people waking up from where they had been sleeping.

Neither India nor I saw what happened to the rickshaw wallah. Afterwards, we were never sure what had occurred. Had he run over something on a street where all manner of things usually lay? Had he braked suddenly? Had someone run into him?

All we knew was that one second we were sitting together in the back seat of the rickshaw, and the next, each of us had been catapulted out either side and on to the ground. I remember so clearly the vertiginous, utterly novel sensation of being propelled through the air; the closest thing I've ever got to flight. We thudded down. Winded, I lay on my back in the street, on the right side of the rickshaw. India lay on its left side. We were both looking up at the sky.

There were two equally fine pieces of luck that shone on us that morning. One, despite the fact that the streets of Delhi were as crowded as they ever were, we were not hit or run over by anything coming after us or, indeed, not thrown directly on to a passing car. Two, we both had our rucksacks strapped on. Our rucksacks acted as a kind of airbag, or giant cushion, protecting both our backs and our heads as we landed at full force on the road, human beetles on our backs.

The rickshaw wallah was looking back at us, frozen and appalled.

'Are you OK?' I called to India.

'I think so,' she called back.

A crowd was gathering. We gingerly got up and inspected each other carefully. Our rucksacks were grubbier than usual as a result of the impact but, otherwise, we were both fine. We got back into the rickshaw, a bit shaken, but far more concerned about possibly missing our bus to Manali due to the unscheduled delay than dwelling on what had just happened.

Manali, high up amid the Kulu Valley mountain range, was snowy enough to go skiing, which I did not, although India did. The cafés and guest houses were lit with candles and food was prepared on kerosene stoves. The houses were made of stone, the air was thin, the roads frequently disappeared under landslides of different sizes. We were cold a lot, wearing all our clothes in layers.

From there, we went to nearby Vashisht. The lodgings were even simpler there and it was even colder. India and I shared a room which was warmed by a stove pipe coming up through the centre of the floor from downstairs. I was extremely glad of her company when, once darkness fell, the many rodents that lived behind the wainscoting started their noisy nocturnal wanderings. I have a pathological fear of rodents, a fear which amused India greatly. I was insistent there not be a scrap of food in our room at any time and was always policing the contents of India's day pack.

'Do you think they might eat their way through the wall in the night?' I asked, only half joking.

'Mice are lovely! Tiny little things.'

'I don't think they're mice,' I said darkly. 'Whatever they are, it's like they're training for the Olympics hundred-metre dash behind those walls. They keep racing up and down. Whatever they are.'

Everything closed even earlier in Vashisht than it had in Manali. With nowhere to go and nothing to do, we went to bed early, lit candles and incense and talked. India told me all about her boyfriend and their up-and-down relationship back in London, which sounded extremely romantic and exciting and grown-up to me.

'The sex is like film sex it's so good,' she said at one point. 'The stuff you see in the movies that you don't think is real, but it is.'

I told her about Jake, the man I had met in Scotland not long before coming travelling, of the *coup de foudre* of our second meeting. Of the letters we wrote to each other. Of the fact that he lived with his girlfriend and my constant struggle to know what was right to do. India in turn listened and asked questions and didn't judge, for which I was grateful.

It was a couple of days before we found out about the thermal pool. It was India who heard about it. I was writing my diary in the warmest café in the village when she came bounding in, zinging with the indefatigable enthusiasm that still defines her.

'Guess what I heard?'

'What?'

'There's a thermal pool here!'

'Where? How come we haven't seen it yet? How do you know?'

The reason we had not been aware of the thermal pool was because it was actually the allocated men's public baths, a place hidden behind high stone walls and a large wooden door.

'I know,' India said with rightful triumph, 'because the woman who runs our guest house is the person who has the key. She goes every night to empty and refill the pool and clean the place for the next morning. She told us we could go there at night when she was finished and she'd give us the key and we could return it for the next morning.'

So that is what we did. We slipped out of our guest house late that moonlit evening, candles in our pockets, and went to the far end of the village, where the men's thermal pool was. The door was unlocked. We went in quietly. What lay behind those walls and the high wooden door was a large rectangular stone pool which had wisps of steam rising from it. The space was roofless, open to the sky. There were temple-like stone carvings set into the walls. Beyond them, the mountains were framed against the moon, a moon whose reflection glittered on the water's surface. We stared around us, enthralled.

'Madame?' It was our guest-house hostess, whispering to us. She held a key out to India. 'Please lock the door when you are finished.' She told us where to put the key in the guest house so she could find it the next morning. And then she went.

This entire place was ours. We went and locked and bolted the door so that nobody else could get in. We lit the candles and stuck them fast to the stone carvings with their own melted wax. Then we stripped off our clothes in the freezing night and slid into the warm thermal waters and swam naked in the moonlight, looking up at the snowy mountains.

'Amazing,' India said.

'I know.'

After that, we didn't bother trying to put it into words. We swam. We leaned against the walls of the pool, staring at the moon. Separately, we meditated on our travels and lives and futures, feeling upheld by the water in the secret hidden pool that had come to us like a gift.

Every night after that, for as long as we remained in Vashisht, we went to lock ourselves into the pool and swim naked under a moon that waxed brighter every night. During the day, we could hear from behind the wall the shouts of the men who occupied it then. But at night, the whole silvery, moonlit, steamy place was our sole preserve. Of all the many experiences I have had while elsewhere, it is this one, which cost nothing, that is one of my most favourite in a lifetime of travels.

Some years ago, I was offered a press trip on a Mediterranean cruise. It was to be for a little more than a week. The ship, the *Ventura*, was to leave Southampton and call at Barcelona, Nice, Rome (or, more correctly, at Civitavecchia port), Ajaccio in Corsica and Gibraltar.

Cruise ships are like arks: the passengers go aboard two by two. It's more efficient to have two to a cabin than one. My trip was for a plus one. I asked India, who was still living in England, if she would like to come. We had remained close friends ever since meeting on our travels, regularly visiting each other.

'I would *love* to come!'

Her son was due back to school at the beginning of the cruise and she first needed a few days to help him settle in. Thus it was arranged that India would fly out to Nice to join the ship there and, meanwhile, I would have a couple of nights on my own.

At the Southampton dock on the appointed day of departure, I was quietly appalled at the size of the ship. It was 19 decks high and 291 metres long. People arrived carrying multiple suitcases; there were to be no fewer than four black-tie dinners on board. The ship took 3,192 passengers and had a crew of 1,220. There were more than 1,500 passenger cabins alone.

As the ship shuddered away from the dock, I took stock of the floating town on which I was now berthed.

Eight restaurants
Nine bars
Five pools
Three show lounges
Circus school
Tennis courts
Spa
Hair salon
Library
Art gallery
Medical centre
Shops

Fourteen of the nineteen decks were public and it took me half a day to orientate myself. The central atrium had a staircase that spiralled downwards and many enormous light features. My shared table in the evening was with three English couples, all friends, who had been cruising together for years. They had nicknames for each other and in-jokes. They told me that on black-tie nights, the tradition was for couples to come down the atrium stairs dressed up and pose for photographs. Where was my partner, one of the women eventually asked over the dessert course on the first night, saying something they had all evidently been thinking.

'My friend is joining me in a couple of days,' I said brightly. In all my years travelling, I had never felt out of place being alone but, on this ship, where everyone travelled in twos, I found myself uncharacteristically ashamed of being by myself.

While waiting for India to arrive, I went to the show lounge that doubled as a cinema to see *Midnight in Paris* and *The King's Speech*. I went to a classical music concert. I investigated the library, which was not worth investigating. I examined the fantastically expensive paintings on sale, one by Rolf Harris for US$65,000, which remained unsold. I ate too much. I sat on my balcony and looked out at the ocean and read my way through the four books I had brought with me by the end of the second day.

In truth, I was both lonely and bored, despite the fact that I could have availed myself of a staggering range of activities, from yoga to crafts and jazz concerts to circus workshops. I also felt tremendously guilty that I was not enjoying myself more and was thinking of all the people who would have loved to have had this opportunity.

Every morning, the ship's newsletter, *Horizon*, was slipped under my door. It listed the activities for that day and the scheduled films and shows. On the morning before India was due to fly to Nice, I picked up the newsletter from the floor and decided I would rouse myself and go to some sociable event.

At 10.30 a.m. that day, a sea day, which meant we would be sailing all day, there was to be a Singles Coffee Morning in the Spinnaker Bar. 'Mingle with other Singles!' the listing chirped. It was the first event I had seen scheduled just for single people and I was cheered to realize there were others in my clan.

I had read Henry James and E. M. Forster and George

Eliot. I knew what a Baedeker was, and what a Grand Tour of Europe had been. Standing there in my cabin that morning, I had a surge of romantic optimism: perhaps some of these single people might be nephews or sons or grandsons accompanying older women relatives on this cruise. That, like Lucy Honeychurch in *A Room with a View*, there might be a George Emerson waiting for me on my journeying. Perhaps their older relative was lying down with a tisane and a scented handkerchief between breakfast and lunch, and this younger and inevitably handsome male relative who was acting as fond companion might also have seen that morning's *Horizon* newsletter with its note about a Singles Coffee Morning at 10.30 a.m.

I arrived to the Spinnaker Bar all smiles, wearing one of my nicest dresses, ready to be sociable and perhaps even courted. I really don't know what I had been thinking. I had been lost in daydreams about some fictional scenario from novels that belonged to an era that pre-dated my own by roughly 150 years.

Not only were there no men at the Singles Coffee Morning of any age, I was the youngest woman there by about thirty years. There were perhaps eight of us who had shown up. I considered departing even before sitting down, but two staff members arrived just then to jolly us along and I was stuck. The members of staff, a young man and a woman, were clearly grappling with gigantic hangovers from the night before, along with a lack of sleep. They made war jokes with each other and drank copious amounts of water and, once the coffee and pastries had arrived, left us to get on with our mingling.

I was sitting beside a woman who was perhaps in her late seventies. She had a very erect posture and was sitting perfectly straight-backed. She wore her hair in tight grey curls. Her brown cardigan was neatly buttoned all the way up to the neck and it matched her brown skirt, which was tweed. The table we were at was low and slightly awkward to navigate. To be polite, I got her a cup and, at her request, poured first tea and then milk.

'Enough!' she snapped, and I stopped pouring the milk, startled at her tone. Her accent was British, something northern I couldn't identify.

She took a plate and piled it with the miniature pastries the kitchen had sent up. The other women in the group were at the far side of the table and already in conversation. There was nobody else near us.

'You're on your own?' she said.

I was desperate to reclaim my non-seaboard life to myself, a life full of company and friends. I was surprised by how much I minded that people might think I was in some way pathetic to be on this cruise alone.

'My friend India is joining me tomorrow,' I said swiftly. 'In Nice. She couldn't get away any earlier.' I drank some coffee. 'You're on your own?' I asked.

The woman finished eating a miniature pastry. She took a sip of tea. 'Didn't arrive on my own, did I?' she said, addressing not me, but the cup.

I was confused. 'Pardon?'

She turned to face me. 'Didn't arrive on my own, did I?' she repeated, but more loudly this time, as if I was having trouble hearing her. 'Husband died, didn't he?'

I thought I had misheard her. 'I'm sorry, what did you just say?'

She looked at me with pity, as if I was both hard of hearing and also pretty dim with it. 'Husband. Died. Didn't. He,' she enunciated, reaching with determination for another pastry.

Two nights previously at dinner, I had heard an announcement over the tannoy calling for a medic to attend a particular cabin. I had guessed it was some kind of coded message of the kind that theatres have if there is a fire in the house, messages intended to alert those who work there, while not panicking the visiting public. But this message had not in fact been in code. While I had been eating my lemon sole and drinking Sauvignon Blanc, medics had been attending this woman's cabin, where her husband had died of a heart attack on the floor.

I was agog at this blunt narration of the death of her husband of more than forty years, a man now dead less than thirty-six hours.

'And where, where is he now?' I managed to say.

She looked at me and jerked her right thumb downwards. In addition to the eight restaurants, nine bars, five pools, and so on, far down in the innards of the ship, somewhere among the five decks which were not publicly accessed, there were three morgue spaces. Her dead husband now lay in one, while she was several decks up, calmly eating pastries at a Singles Coffee Morning. Wildly, I looked across at the rest of our little group. They had heard nothing of our conversation.

'And are you OK?' I managed. 'Are the crew looking after you?' And then, 'Have you told your family?'

They had had no children and there was no family to be told.

'There's neighbours, but we keep ourselves to ourselves. There's Marion, a girl I used to work with until we both retired. We have lunch once a fortnight, every second Friday. I'll tell

Marion at our next lunch. She will want to hear all about the cruise.'

'Will the crew be flying you home from Nice?' I asked. It seemed an unbearable prospect to me, to be trapped on a ship with your dead spouse and to have to wait another day to disembark.

The ship's company had indeed offered to repatriate both her and the body back to England from Nice. She had refused.

'Always wanted to see Rome, didn't I?' she said, fixing me with a glare. 'Been looking forward to this cruise for a long time, haven't I?'

And so, she would be staying on board for the remaining days, she in the cabin they had both occupied on arrival and her husband in cold storage several decks down.

The following day, India arrived and rescued me from my ennui. I told her the story, of course, immediately. She was horrified.

'Let's see if you can find her, and maybe we can have lunch with her. She must still be in shock,' India said.

I did not, in fact, think that the woman whose husband had died had been in shock. She had seemed unnervingly well composed to me. As it turned out, I never did see her again in the coming days. The ship was so large, and the passengers were so many. I kept looking out for her but could not spot her anywhere. India and I wondered aloud from time to time how she was coping, and if Rome, which she had always wanted to see, had lived up to her expectations.

On the final morning, I was disembarked early at South-ampton, as I had a flight to catch. As I turned back to wave to India, who was hanging over our balcony, something caught my eye. It was a hearse, parked discreetly further down on the pier. I saw a coffin being put into it. And then I saw the recently bereaved woman get into the front seat with the driver, and they drove away slowly, back to her life in some northern city that had changed for ever.

When we met in 1995, both India and I assumed that our future lives would involve weddings, husbands and children in some form, if not necessarily in that order. That is not how things worked out. Between the two of us, there has been one engagement (mine), no weddings and only one child (hers), now a smart and handsome teenager.

For much of Bryn's life, India has raised him as a single parent. This had not been her plan. All of the challenges and joys that come with being a parent, she has gone through by herself. It wasn't what she had wanted, no more than not being a parent was what I ever wanted.

When Bryn turned two, India felt ready to leave him in the care of her mother for a couple of nights. It was the first time she had been away from him overnight. The two of us met up in Madrid for a weekend, a city neither of us had ever been to before. It's a momentous thing when a parent leaves their child overnight for the first time and I was extremely touched it was me whom India wanted to spend that landmark time with. We stayed in the centre of Madrid, in a hotel in an old building. Our room was five storeys up and had a tiny balcony.

On the Saturday, we saw the startlingly lush paintings by Velázquez in the Prado. Neither of us had realized how huge the canvases were, so gigantic, it felt as though, if we stood there long enough, we would be swallowed up and transported back to rooms four centuries old. We went from there to the Reina Sofia and saw Picasso's *Guernica*, its 1930s cubism frying our heads; the time-travelling we were doing in one day with artists born centuries apart was so intense we both felt like a lie-down afterwards to absorb it all.

We didn't do that, though. Free time for herself was the scarcest thing in India's life just then and, indeed, still is. She wanted to get as much as possible out of our precious weekend together in Madrid. So we walked in the beautifully atmospheric El Retiro Park, with its fountains and ornamental lakes. We browsed at the El Rastro flea market, marvelling at the vast china tureens and vintage army uniforms and immense chandeliers missing strands of crystals.

I bought a small photograph album which had tissue-paper leaves in between each page. There were no people in the sepia photographs. Each one had been taken in the same back garden, of a different tablecloth with handmade cotton lace around the border, displayed on a washing line. There was a woman's hand in the bottom right of each photograph, holding the cloth steady. She must have made these to sell and taken pictures of them before they were sold. Did she keep any for herself? I wondered. Was this how she had made her living? How had this album ended up in a flea market?

We went to a range of cafés and bars throughout the weekend. We ate anchovies and sardines and fried squid and patatas bravas and churros and drank a lot of wine. We talked and talked.

'This is who I used to be,' India said at one point. 'I don't get to do this any more. Galleries. Culture. Travelling. Spending hours in a bar. Talking to adults.'

India wasn't complaining. She was just stating a fact. Her life was different now that her beloved Bryn was in it, a child she had sole responsibility for almost all of the time. Her time was not her own any more. Her life had changed for ever.

In the years that followed, I longed for my own life to change in the same way, for parenthood. It didn't happen. India longed for another child. That didn't happen either. In the strangest of ways, we see in each other how our lives would have been if the opposite had happened to each of us: if it had been me who had had the child and India was the one who remained free to do anything she pleased at short notice and travel where she wished. We have seen in some ways our alternate life journeys represented by the other.

The truth is, we have both always wanted what the other now has. We both wanted to be parents. In parenthood, we both wanted to retain at least some of the things that gave us joy in our single lives, especially travel and a certain amount of freedom. We both wanted to be married. Neither of us ever wanted to raise a child without the full-time support of a life partner, preferably a husband, who was also preferably the child's father. None of that turned out the way we wanted.

India and I ended up on two very different life paths, although we started out on the same one when we first met in India, all those years ago. She has her son. I have my freedom. Sometimes, I can't help wondering which of us has the better life. But it's an impossible question to answer, and an irrelevant one too. The truth is, we can only know the one life we actually have.

There is another important truth, though: I have learned it's possible to also live vicariously through the different lives of those friends we love, to look through lit windows and enter the open doors that lead into the lives we don't have ourselves. And that vicariousness, which India and I now have with each other, is something to be cherished very dearly.

LOST FRIENDS

I DON'T KNOW how many friends I've lost over a lifetime. Dozens. Scores. There is a class photograph stuck in a book in my house from the year we were ten together. We are lined up on stone steps in the garden of the convent, a garden that is now the town's supermarket car park. These are the girls I spent years with; in our primary school, you stayed in the same class for your entire education there. I can remember some of their names. Fiona. Catherine. Eve. Maura. Martina. Mary. Ursula.

Not a single one of them stayed in my life. Nor did any of the fellow boarders who sustained me through six years of boarding school. Catriona. Deirdre. Mia. Dervilla. Nessa. Aideen. Susan. Two Margarets. Another Fiona. Patricia. Franziska. Vanessa. We helped each other navigate our teenage years while mainly enclosed in a convent from which most of us left only one weekend a month or for the holidays. We knew everything about the minutiae of each other's school lives: what posters we had Blu-tacked to our cubicle walls; who snored at night; who never ate the mash and fried eggs served up for dinner each Friday night; who got up every morning for 7.30 Mass; whose parents had failed to tell them the facts of life, or about periods, before arrival at the school.

Our real homes were scattered all over Ireland. It seems so strange to me now to realize that I never saw most of those other homes, never saw those parents and siblings and houses and gardens and pets that were the unseen matrix of our other lives. We spent so much time together at school that we rarely went to visit each other during holidays. We lived like sisters and yet so much of our lives were mysteries beyond the scaffolding of the routines and the timetable that began with a nun ringing a bell in the dormitory at seven each morning and ended with another nun switching lights off at ten each night.

These friends, too, all vanished eventually. Some emigrated. Others I simply lost touch with. Much of it was deliberate on my part: I had hated those boarding-school years so much I did not want to be reminded of it in any way. Even when some of these friends got in touch later in life when the internet arrived, via email or social media, I mostly ignored the overtures. To this day, I have not attended a single class reunion.

I didn't realize until starting to write this how much I regret all that now. These were hugely important friends who supported, encouraged and counselled me in so many different ways for six years. Irreplaceable friends with whom I shared so much. Plus, I really, really liked those girls. We lived together so closely for those formative years, aged twelve to eighteen, that we should have – I should have – been invested in, curious about and proactive in discovering how our lives turned out afterwards.

But I didn't. I let them all become lost.

It was more or less the same with the few friends I managed to make during my college years. I spent three of those four years engaged in studying a subject it soon became clear to me that I had almost no interest in – history – yet failing to do anything about switching to something else. What I should have done was drop out of university entirely. Having realized very quickly I did not have a gift for academia, I then wasted the following years endlessly regretting not having applied for the journalism course in the College of Commerce in Rathmines. I also spent three of those four years uselessly enthralled by a fellow student whose girlfriend I longed to be.

In the same way I had let go my boarding-school friends because I associated them with an education and a place I had loathed, I swiftly moved away from university friends once I'd graduated. They were to me reminders only of wasted time and failure: of failure to have had the courage to admit having made a huge mistake in my choice of a third-level course and college; and the wasted time in not realizing earlier that the man I thought I was in love with was never going to be interested in having me as his girlfriend.

Back then, I thought I had ruined my life before it had even started, both career-wise and relationship-wise, and so I wanted nothing in my future to remind me of these two mistakes. I know it sounds crazy now, but when you are twenty-one, your life choices feel very intense, or at least they did to me. It took years before I even walked through that campus again, although to do so was to make a significant short cut to our *Irish Times* office.

So I lost all the friends I made throughout my entire education, by my own choice.

There have been other losses along the way, but much smaller ones. The friends you meet travelling, spend some time with and then never see again. I look back at my diaries and puzzle over names. Who was Diana and her partner, Alan, whom I met in Sydney and went to the Blue Mountains for a weekend with? I cannot recall a single thing about them.

Who were the people who wrote their names and addresses at the back of my guidebooks, urging me to keep in touch with them? Who the hell were Steve and Finn and Daisy and Fernanda and Lucius? They have all written their names at the back of my *Lonely Planet India*, and I have no idea where I met them, or what we did together, or anything about them. But clearly, we liked each other enough to want to stay in touch. Except we never did.

And then there are the really big losses: the friends who leave you. Those friends whom you never wanted to lose, or ever thought such a thing was possible. Yet they left us. Each decade, I have lost one extremely important friendship, people I thought would be in my life for ever. People I knew I'd never be finished talking to. Friends I loved, and who certainly loved me too. But still I lost them. Love is not always enough to sustain a platonic friendship, just as it is not with a sexual relationship. Sometimes, the unavoidable truth is, our friends just leave us. I don't know how many other people out there have had a similar experience of being left by a friend, but I can't be the only one.

In my twenties, when I lived in London, I had a very close friend whose friendship endured even when I went travelling for long periods or went back and forth to Ireland. I'll call him Rupert. We were always going for drinks and dinners and roaming around museums and galleries together. I loved his company. He told me he loved mine. When apart, he wrote me many letters.

When I was living back in Dublin for a while, a couple of years after Rupert and I had first met, I discovered my then boyfriend had been cheating on me. I found out because we went for a walk, I got cold and he loaned me his jacket. I was still cold, so I put my hands in the pockets and discovered a recently used condom, which had not been used by us.

Considering what an asshole this man was, I grieved over him far too much after dumping him. About a week after my discovery of the used condom, I collected a stack of 50-pence pieces, went to a public phone box and called Rupert in London, sobbing throughout the call.

A couple of days later, a fat envelope arrived to my house-share. It was from Rupert and it contained a veritable lucky bag of tiny, beautiful things, a kind of paper cabinet of curiosities. There was an orange fabric bracelet with yellow smiley faces and the words 'Don't Worry, Be Happy, Don't Worry'. There was an Italian banknote for 2,000 lire. There was an iron-on badge from NASA. There were some old cigarette cards, each depicting a different river valley in Britain: Nuneham, Aberglaslyn, Sunbury. There was a shiny metallic gold star. There were cut-outs of bright butterflies.

There was a little thing that had come out of a box of cornflakes: a 'Magic Window', a picture of birds which, when you pulled a tab to make it slide, transformed from black and white to colour. There were many old red postal stickers, all saying 'Special'. There was a piece of brown hard cardboard, cut from something larger, which had these words: 'As the Jolly Man Said, Enjoy It Now, Because You'll Be a Long Time Dead.' There was also a long letter from Rupert, full of wise counsel. I was so touched by his thoughtfulness and the trouble he had gone to to amass these things for my diversion that I cried again.

I went on to spend many more happy times with Rupert, who even came to visit me in Dublin. (Rupert and I were ourselves never candidates for a relationship: he was gay.) We were the closest of friends for years. I flew to London, at some expense, specially to celebrate his thirtieth birthday. I believed our friendship was wonderful, and wonderfully uncomplicated. Until he decided overnight that he was offended by me.

I know this, because he told me so, the last time I ever saw him, in a café near Brick Lane. What offended him? Well, my love of travel and what he described as my 'lack of ambition' as a result of travelling. That was mentioned. It was true I worked short-term jobs back then that offered no career prospects, solely so I could travel a lot, for no higher purpose than to exercise my curiosity. I had not thought this was the business of anyone else except myself. Apparently, this had offended Rupert, who also called me a 'ridiculous tourist'.

My less than positive feedback to something he had written that was scheduled to be in the public domain the following year? That was mentioned too. I had thought I was being helpful, that trusted friends can speak important truths to each other. It appeared they could not; not in this case, anyway. Rupert had been specifically offended by this feedback of mine, by what he described as my 'embarrassing disloyalty'.

'You need to grow up,' he told me, over our cold Earl Grey pot of tea, and muffins neither of us had touched. I was twenty-eight. 'Go away and don't get in contact again until you've stopped travelling like a tourist, and when you have something to say.'

He actually said all that. Someone who had been a beloved friend for years said all that to me. I remember it so well because I've never been able to forget it.

I was so shocked I didn't say anything. All I could think in that moment was: is he right? Is my life as shallow as this? Am I a humiliating embarrassment? Have I been a terrible friend to him? I sat there in dazed silence and public humiliation, feeling profoundly, profoundly hurt. Then I got up and walked out of the café and left him there with the cold tea and uneaten muffins. That was the last time I ever saw Rupert.

For ages afterwards, I tried to make sense of what had happened, but none of it made sense to me. He never apologized. He never contacted me again. Rupert vanished from my life, literally overnight. I guess I already knew when walking out of that café that our friendship was completely over, ruined for ever. I had not the smallest wish to see him again. You can't ever come back from someone you have trusted with intimate details about your personal life then telling you that your life – your entire existence, your values – now offends them.

I kept his many letters and cards, including the beautiful one packed with kindness that he sent after I realized my boyfriend was cheating on me. I have the piece of cardboard stating that the-jolly-man-instructs-life-should-be-enjoyed-now-because-we'll-all-be-dead-eventually, stuck into the mirror over my fireplace. I don't know why I have kept all these things. Evidence that Rupert and I were once friends? Evidence to whom? Myself?

The mystery of our friendship itself remains. How could I have been so close to this person for so long and not have known our connection was in truth so fragile? How could my former friend not only treat me so badly but state such devastatingly hurtful comments at what was essentially my exit interview? It is decades now since I have seen Rupert and yet the loss of our friendship puzzles me still and probably always will.

In my thirties, a friend I had had for many years slowly disappeared into mental illness, a friend so close for so long he had felt as familiar to me as one of my own limbs. I called him my brother. He called me his sister. Like someone being sucked into a bog or gradually dragged underwater, that person went away, little by little, and was eventually transformed into someone I no longer knew, like the changeling in fairy tales.

I tried so hard to rescue him. I lay flat on the surface of the bog and reached out a hand, a stick, a ladder. I threw lifebelts into the water. I launched boats. I even tried to swim out and save him, but I had to retreat when he attempted to pull me under with him. That friendship had to end, although I am not sure who left who in the end. He has been irretrievably lost to me ever since.

In my forties, a friend of almost twenty years and who lived in another country dropped me. She and I had been to each other's homes in our respective countries scores of times. We had had so much fun, shared so many book recommendations, cooked and eaten so many amazing meals together, talked so often at length about so many things, sent so many letters and cards and gifts to each other and been through some terrible life-changing experiences together. At some point, I assumed that we would be friends for ever. No, I didn't assume. I was certain.

But that is not what happened. What happened was . . . what did happen? Even now, I don't really know. This is maybe fifteen years ago now. I only know she decided never to talk to me again, without ever discussing it with me. It must have been my fault, but when you don't know what you have done – or are too lacking in self-awareness to figure it out for yourself – it's almost impossible to know how to fix it.

Besides, the other person may not want to fix it. When the

relationship is not sexual or romantic, or does not involve shared responsibilities for children, or shared finances, or property, or anything except the voluntary frivolity of simply enjoying each other's company, there is no granular reason to work through a breakdown in communication. People can just walk away and never look back, never address the discomfort or pain unwittingly caused by the other. Which is exactly what happened with this person.

There is a story I came across not long ago, the story of a lost Leonardo da Vinci drawing being found in 1998. It was a sketch of Orpheus, the musician in the Greek myths, being attacked by the Furies. The da Vinci expert who discovered it, Carlo Pedretti, believed that it was a page that had come from the *Codex*, da Vinci's notebook of his observations and theories on a number of topics. The sensational discovery of the lost da Vinci drawing made international news.

The drawing was then sent for restoration. And . . . it vanished. The restoration team used water and alcohol on it without first testing the ink of the drawing for solubility. Thus the ink drawing simply started to steadily fade away, until it had dissolved completely. Instead of restoring the Leonardo da Vinci drawing, lost for an unknown number of centuries, they made it disappear again within just three years. I cannot even begin to imagine the horror that would have slowly descended on the restoration team as they watched a work of art worth millions literally unmake itself in front of them: the very reverse of creation – destruction.

In 2001, Carlo Pedretti broke the news of the disaster to an Italian newspaper. 'I will not say where it happened or whose fault it was.' He hoped, he said, that 'chemical experiments might recover the lost image, but the damage was irreversible'.

When I read that story, it made me think of that lost friendship from my forties. Something wonderful and precious that had been years in the creation just vanished. Disappeared. All that was left of the da Vinci was the paper the drawing had been made on; all that was left of that particular friendship was memories and the gifts, cards and letters we had exchanged and which I still have. I still feel confused and, in some inexplicable way, ashamed about that lost friendship.

For several years, I hoped that someday my phone might ring, or an email appear, or a letter arrive: a chance to rebuild a friendship I had thought I had cherished so much but, clearly, had not cherished enough. I don't have that hope any more. It's too long ago now. We might recover a faint image of that friendship we once had together, but the damage is irreversible.

I think about all these different lost friends more and more as time passes.

THE ESSENTIAL FRIEND

THE DISUSED LIBRARY was close to a back stairway in the boarding school I attended in the Midlands. It did not have anyone supervising it and nobody ever checked out the books because nobody ever borrowed them. There were volumes of yearbooks from an American high school that our convent order had some association with. There were religious books, sets of ancient encyclopaedias, bound copies of religious magazines. It was more a storeroom for books that nobody wanted any more, or knew what to do with; long ago, it had been the library that served the boarding school, before it expanded and built a whole new campus for day pupils, including a library with books that young girls actually wanted to read.

The boarding school was large and the disused library was rarely visited. I liked its moribund silence and the privacy it afforded in an environment where it was hard to find privacy. I sometimes went there to escape the general clamour.

One afternoon, I noticed the spine of a book I could not remember seeing before. It was high up on a shelf close to the ceiling, a hardback with a pale yellow spine and the title *A Night to Remember*. I was seventeen and held out some faint hope that it might perhaps be a racy romantic novel, a novel that had somehow eluded the notice of the nuns. I stood on a chair and took the book down.

A Night to Remember was not a romantic novel. It was

Walter Lord's famous 1955 book about the sinking of the *Titanic* in 1912. I opened up the book. It was a third printing, dated December 1955; the other two were November 1955 and also December 1955. The publisher was Henry Holt of New York. When I turned the pages, an undated letter written on lined notepaper fell out. I picked it up. It was written in untidy blue biro.

I sat down with the book and looked at it properly. Whoever had written the letter had also written something on the title page: 'The property of Eugene P. Daly, survivor of the ill-fated *Titanic*, 15th of April 1912.' On another page was a small black-and-white photograph of a man in a tweed cap in front of a house. 'A photo of Eugene Daly, *Titanic* survivor.' At the back of the book, he had marked his name on the passenger list, along with an address in Athlone. The passenger list was reproduced and the names of those who survived were in italics, as his was.

The letter had a Galway city address and was addressed simply to 'A Chara'.

> As I have promised this is the book of the Disaster of 1912. You will see my name in the list of 3rd Class at the end marked in ink.
>
> You need not rush in returning it. Give time for all your community who wish to read it.
>
> May God prosper you and reward you in your work.
>
> Sincerely yours
>
> Eugene Daly

I knew, of course, that the 'unsinkable' *Titanic* had been built in Belfast and sank on its first voyage across the Atlantic. Many people had died and the ship had ever since lain undiscovered in the deep waters of the unexplored Atlantic. I read the letter again. Eugene Daly must have sent it and the book to an unnamed nun in my boarding school, back in the 1950s. This nun must have been known to him and his family. Whoever she was, she had heeded his request about not hurrying to return the book. She had in fact never returned it to him and, somehow, it had ended up in this disused library decades later, forgotten until I found it.

I took the book back to my dormitory and started to read it. Within minutes, I was gripped, utterly compelled by A *Night to Remember,* feeling I was actually there on board the doomed ship on that icy April evening as chaos unfolded everywhere to its inevitable end. Lord had interviewed sixty-three survivors and pieced together the story of the last day and night by jigsawing their stories together, along with a considerable amount of background research.

Against the broad sweep of the narrative itself, it was the details that stayed with me. The First Class 'Luncheon' menu on the last day at sea: cock-a-leekie, fillets of brill, grilled mutton chops, Norwegian anchovies, veal-and-ham pie, brawn, corned ox tongue, and much, much more. The random items people wanted to take with them on to lifeboats when, so very soon, it would become clear that hundreds of other people were dying in the water. A toy pig that played something called the maxixe when its tail was turned. A Bible. The book a man had been reading in bed before the commotion began. Three oranges. A Pomeranian pet dog. An ivory miniature. A velvet bag of jewels.

And all the stuff left behind to sink to the bottom of the ocean. A jewelled copy of the *Rubaiyat of Omar Khayyam,* its golden cover set with one thousand emeralds, rubies, amethysts and topazes. Five Steinway grand pianos. Eight hundred cases of shelled walnuts. Sixteen trunks of clothes belonging to one couple alone. A chest of china bound for Tiffany's. A silver duck press. Twelve cases of ostrich plumes. Unknown quantities of diamonds. A case of gloves. Thirty thousand eggs. A Renault Coupe de Ville, the only car on board. A handwritten manuscript by Joseph Conrad. Thousands of bottles of champagne.

Then there were all the characters. The older couple in First Class, the Strauses, who would not be parted, even though both were offered places in a lifeboat, and who both chose to remain on deck. Bruce Ismay, chairman of the White Star Line, who survived and was doomed to be savaged by all in the years to come. Captain Edward J. Smith, who may or may not have had a part in the whole disaster by ignoring the ice warnings, who knew, as the ship began to sink, that the *Titanic* held only twenty lifeboats, with space for 1,178 at full capacity, who knew there were more than 2,220 people aboard.

Although an Irish teenager myself when I first read *A Night to Remember*, I did not identify with my young Irish peers emigrating in Third Class. It barely registered with me then that the stories of my own kinspeople, the Irish on the *Titanic*, were largely unrecorded in the book. Down in Steerage and left to find their own way up to the higher decks and to the lifeboats, the majority of them drowned. They had no staterooms for stewards to knock on, to alert them to dress and put on life jackets and direct them to the lifeboats.

For all the talk about 'women and children first', Lord noted that the death rate for Third Class children was higher than it was for First Class men. Of the 706 Third Class passengers aboard, only 178 survived: 75 men, 76 women and 27 children. Eugene Daly, whose book, letter and photograph I now had, was one of these 75 men. The passenger list showed him as embarking at Cobh, then Queenstown.

No, when I first read *A Night to Remember,* I placed myself squarely among the members of the privileged First Class, taking on different personas as I read. Variously, I was the Countess of Rothes, who handled the tiller of Lifeboat B and helped keep everyone's spirits up. Or Madeleine Astor, just one year older than me, the pregnant wife of millionaire John Jacob Astor IV and returning from an Egyptian honeymoon. They had boarded at Cherbourg, along with a valet, her maid, a nurse and Kitty, her husband's pet Airedale dog. Her husband put her into Lifeboat 4 while he remained aboard to die. Or I was Molly Brown, in Lifeboat 6, taking an oar and trying unsuccessfully to persuade the occupants of the boat that they must go back to try to rescue people calling to them as they drowned all around them. I wanted not just to survive the disaster but to be glamorous and heroic in my survival.

The book made such an impression on me and I was so beguiled by the *Titanic* story and by the extravagance of its tragedy that I decided to write to Walter Lord and tell him so. He might, I thought, be interested in the letter I had found in the book. And, I thought, with the self-absorption of a teenager, perhaps I might coax him into giving me a piece of *Titanic* memorabilia from a collection I was quite certain he had to have after all those interviews he had done.

On 4 January 1983, I duly wrote a letter to him, care of 'Henry Holt and Company, New York, USA'. It seems absolutely astonishing to me now that I had a personal reply within a month, a typed and hand-signed aerogramme dated 29 January with an address from East 68th Street, New York, N.Y. 10021.

Dear Rosita

I am glad you enjoyed A Night to Remember *and flattered that it seems to have made such an impression on you.*

Thank you for sending me the Xerox of that interesting letter you found inside the book. I, too, feel sure it is genuine. He included his address, so why don't you try writing him direct on the chance that he is still alive? After all, many of those young Irish boys and girls were still in their teens, and he could easily be still in his 80s today.

Yes, I do have a few odds and ends from the Titanic – mostly small personal items carried off the ship and given me later by survivors – but you are right: I value them very highly and wouldn't think of parting with them, even when the request comes from such a talented and persuasive writer as yourself.

Warm regards
Walter Lord

On the back of the aerogramme he wrote a PS. *Delighted to send you the address of the* Titanic *Historical Society. It's:* Titanic Historical Society, Box 53, Indian Orchard, Massachusetts 01151.

Walter Lord's letter thrilled me for weeks, months. I still have it, folded carefully into his own book, along with Eugene Daly's letter.

When I left school later that year, I took the book with me. I guess you could say I purloined it from the disused library. By then, I had indeed written to the Galway address in Eugene Daly's letter but, this time, there had been no reply. Then, two years later, in September 1985, the location of the wreck was discovered in a joint expedition by the US Navy and Robert Ballard, an oceanographer.

The world learned that the *Titanic* lay almost four kilometres underwater in the Atlantic, and 600 kilometres from the nearest landmass, at Newfoundland. Images came back from the deep, taken of the exterior of the shattered ship. But it was the pictures that were taken on Ballard's expedition the following year, in July 1986, that caused a true international sensation.

These pictures were from the ship's interior and the vast debris trail that lay between the two locations of the ship, which had broken in half as it sank. They showed an intact lopsided crystal chandelier with sea-creatures perched upon it like marine feathers, still suspended from its brass chain. They showed gleaming brass fittings; the ship's wheel, minus its wood; lifeboat-launching winches; portholes; safes; unbroken bottles of champagne; white unbroken dishes; a copper hip bath. They did not show any human remains: long claimed by nature.

I pored over these eerie images and the newspaper stories of the expedition, absolutely agog. It was like staring into the past, like time-travelling. Now I could see for myself a little of what the passengers in Walter Lord's book had seen. It seemed fantastical to me that anything had survived intact at all after so long under the water. The image of the chandelier, in particular, swung in my head for a long, long time.

I first met my friend Jon when I was a student, way back. His best friend was going out with one of my flatmates. He was someone on the periphery of my student life. He went to a different college. I don't recall ever meeting him one on one. Like many other shadowy people from that time, he was someone occasionally in the background, whom I never saw again once we graduated. Jon studied marketing and I was vaguely aware that he had gone away from Ireland after college.

One day, when I was not long back in Ireland myself after several years wandering the world, and working at the *Irish Times*, I received an email from Jon. It took me a minute or two to figure out who he was and how he had fitted into my past. He told me that he had recently come back to Ireland after many years working abroad and was making contact with people he used to know.

'Would you like to meet for dinner?' he wrote at the end of the email.

I rummaged in my memory for a single conversation I had had with Jon way back in our student days. Nope. Nothing. I could not even recall what he looked like. I admired the way he had tracked me down, though; this was long before Facebook or any other kind of social media.

I agreed to meet for dinner. It was just one dinner is how I looked at it. If we had nothing to talk about, there was no need to ever meet him again.

As it happened, we did find many things to talk about. We were different people then to who we had been in college. Over that first dinner, we connected immediately in a way that both of us found surprising but was also somehow entirely natural in its wholly unexpected ease and intimacy. Jon told me about his heartbreak from recently being dumped by his boyfriend. I knew about heartbreak. We shared our heartbreak stories. We laughed over a bottle of wine like co-conspirators against the shittiness of our lives right then. I came away from that dinner buzzing, knowing I had made an important new friend.

That was some twenty years ago. Almost at once, Jon became a very close friend and has remained so ever since. He is my go-to person when I need advice. There is probably no major decision I have made in the last two decades that hasn't first involved a consultation with him. Whether it's advice on a work matter or a personal one, he always has something wise to say or some observation I would never have figured out by myself. There are very few people who can offer equally valuable counsel on matters both professional and personal, but Jon is one of them.

My wise friend sees things I can't. I am far too impetuous and tend to go off like a rocket-fuelled kite when I get exercised about something, not taking the time to calmly consider the wider picture. I am all unconsidered reaction. Jon is analytical where I am intuitive. He is the one down on the ground, casually winding my wildly climbing kite self back down out of danger. We all need a friend like that, to save us from ourselves – or, at least, I certainly do.

One of the things I love most about our friendship is the fact that we have similar obsessions. He was already fixated on the *Titanic* by the time I met him and knew almost as much about it as I did. I showed him my book and the letters from Walter Lord and Eugene Daly and he turned their pages in my kitchen with a kind of reverence. Whenever a particular story becomes news, we are both united in being all over the detail. We find every rabbit hole in every story and we spend a long time down there together. We become so deeply invested in stories, they almost become part of our sensibility and consciousness. From time to time, we tell each other we are going to make a podcast together called 'In the Detail', in which we discuss our current obsession, because there is always one.

When the Malaysian Airlines Flight 370 went missing in 2014, we texted and talked for hours and days and weeks about our theories of what had happened to it. When Sheryl Sandberg's husband, Dave Goldberg, fell off a treadmill in a gym in Mexico and died, there was no conspiracy theory we did not ventilate as to how it had happened. When Oscar Pistorius was on trial for the shooting of Reeva Steenkamp, it's a flat-out miracle either of us ever got any work done, so closely did we follow the trial in real time, texting each other throughout, sharing floorplans and photographs of his apartment and of the shattered bathroom door, and of transcripts of interviews with the neighbours. We are inexhaustible in our obsessions; we outlast everyone else.

I recommended Jon Krakauer's *Into the Wild* to my Jon, and on the day he read it he was sending me YouTube links to footage of the infamous Alaskan bus where Chris McCandless died in 1992. During the pandemic, the bus was airlifted from its location to an as yet unknown destination because people had died in their attempts to make a pilgrimage to see it and many others had had to be rescued. I saw the story on Twitter and at once forwarded to Jon the video of the bus suspended over the Denali forest Chris McCandless could not find his way out of. It stirred and moved me in a particular way that I knew, of all my friends, only Jon would understand, because the story had stirred and moved him too. But it was about more than that too, about making some acknowledgement to each other again of Chris McCandless's life, of remembering the man who had died alone in the bus.

It was Jon who introduced me to the story of the Lost Girls of Panama and, since then, I have read as much as I can find on this story of the two young Dutch girls who disappeared while hiking in 2014. Kris Kremers and Lisanne Froon were twenty-one and twenty-two when they vanished in Panama, where they had gone to learn Spanish. Fragments of their body parts were found months later, along with Lisanne's camera, which had ninety flash photographs taken at night in the jungle and time-stamped a week after they vanished. It is still unclear what happened to them.

'I think the reason it haunts me so much,' Jon said when he first put me on to this story, 'is the fact that so many of us have been adventurous when we were in our twenties and thought nothing of taking risks.' Both Jon and I have travelled extensively, starting when we were in our twenties, and we both took risks, risks that I don't think I'd take now. 'That could have been us,' as he says. Their story haunts me too now. Kris and Lisanne went out in the world, travelling, full of life and seeking adventures in a new country and a new culture, as we did at their age. The difference is that they never made it back from their adventure.

When James Cameron's movie *Titanic* came out in 1997, I saw it in a cinema in Edinburgh with Jake, my partner at the time. It was spectacle from start to finish. Walter Lord had been a consultant on the movie; a black-and-white documentary-style movie based on his own book had come out in 1958. James Cameron famously inserted the fictional Jack-and-Rose romance into his movie storyline but, in the cinema that night, it was the story of Ida and Isidor Straus that made the biggest impression on me.

In real life, the Strauses, who were co-owners of Macy's department store in New York, were First Class passengers. Ida was sixty-three and Isidor sixty-seven. They had spent the winter of 1911 and the early months of 1912 touring Europe. They had not intended to sail back to New York on the *Titanic*.

A coal strike in England at that time meant that supplies intended for other ships were diverted to the *Titanic* and so they booked that ship instead. By such extraneous happenings are fates shaped.

The classic, much-reproduced photograph of the Strauses, which is also included in Lord's book, is a formal studio picture. It's black and white. Ida sits in a dark dress with long sleeves, holding a chatelaine-type chain. Her hair is formally rolled back from her face. She's looking off to the side, neither smiling nor frowning, slightly aloof.

Isidor Straus is perched on the right arm of the chair his wife is sitting in. He's in a black suit, with cufflinks visible on his white shirt, a gleaming tie loosely knotted under a wing collar. He is bald and has a neat beard and round, wire-rimmed glasses. He looks calm and grave.

Ida Straus had a maid with her on the *Titanic*, Ellen Bird, whom she had engaged in London prior to sailing from Southampton. On the night the iceberg struck, the Straus couple were seen on deck, near Lifeboat 8, along with Ellen Bird. In the hours when a form of odd chivalrous civility still pertained, before the realization that the ship was really sinking in the dark night and it was every man, woman and child for themselves, Isidor Straus refused to take a place in Lifeboat 8, along with his wife and her maid. At that point, in some lifeboats at least, it was still women and children first.

Lord has witnesses recalling Ida saying this: 'We have been living together for many years. Where you go, I go.'

Whatever it was she said, Ida Straus did not take her place in the lifeboat. She took off her fur coat and gave it to her maid, who did get into Lifeboat 8. In the eyewitness accounts

Lord gathered, the couple then sat down on deckchairs on A deck to await their fate.

In Cameron's movie, the couple go back to their stateroom. They lie on their bed together, atop a quilted eiderdown, holding on to each other silently. The scene is shot from above and you begin to gradually notice the water that comes slowly lapping in under the door and then in under their bed, and then the shot fades away.

I could never understand why Ida Straus did not get into a lifeboat. It didn't matter whether she awaited death from a deckchair or in her stateroom cabin. The point was, she had a choice that so few others had on that night. I could not, and do not, understand why you would not want to save yourself from certain death, why you would not want to survive.

Watching the movie in the Edinburgh cinema, I wanted Ida Straus to leap out of that bed before the water arrived and run from the room, husband or no husband. As people wept and sniffed into handkerchiefs around me in the cinema, I was full of fury, desperately willing Ida to try to find a lifeboat that would take her to safety instead of lying there, waiting passively for death. Why was she sacrificing herself? To me, there was nothing romantic in her decision. I thought she was out of her mind.

In actuality, Isidor Straus's body was found and recovered. Ida's was not, lost for ever in the Atlantic. In burial at least, they were not destined to be together.

Sometime in 2011, I had an email from Jon. It was an invitation to a party, a full year hence, at his home. Jon throws great parties. I opened the mail with anticipation.

Party on Saturday, 14 April 2012

The Titanic hit an iceberg at 23h40 on 14 April 1912. As we know, Jack and Rose were on deck. At 02.20 on 15 April 1912, the ocean liner sank. Happily, Rose and most of the other First Class passengers were saved.

This gives you one year to plan your costume.

Come dressed as a ship/a lifeboat/the unsinkable Molly Brown/Jack/ Rose/the Captain/an enterprising Third Class waif/ an iceberg/Lady Astor (pregnant)/Celine Dion/the North Atlantic/ a deckchair/a rat/a cross-dressing survivor/anything else of an appropriate Titanical theme.

Warning: those arriving without costume risk the wrath of the host and will likely be thrown overboard.

There were two pictures with the invite, a drawing of the real *Titanic* sinking and one of Leonardo DiCaprio and Kate Winslet in their infamously cheesy scene at the prow of the ship where she's holding out her arms, pretending to fly.

I was appalled. I thought this proposed party, a year hence, was in the worst possible taste. I could hardly believe that my smart, funny, wise friend was planning such a crass travesty of an event.

'Is this a joke?' I mailed back. 'People died! Hundreds of them. It's not funny!'

Jon had no time at all for my accusations of bad taste. He just laughed at me. He even got a bit annoyed when I told him off and announced that I would definitely, absolutely, a hundred per cent not be attending. I brought it up several times when next we met. 'Don't come if you don't want to come,' he told me finally.

He thought a century was long enough to be satirical about a historical event, whereas I thought some things were beyond satire. True, the party was also to be a fundraiser for the RNLI, but the untapped puritan in me wondered if they would want to accept the money if they knew the circumstances in which it had been raised.

As the year wore on, I received more than one reminder about Jon's *Titanic*-themed party, which I ignored.

I am not sure at what point I decided that I would, in fact, go. It was partly about not wanting to be left out. Partly because I was questioning my own uptightness about what was, after all, a party. At any rate, I changed my mind, very much to Jon's amusement. He enquired as to what I would come dressed as.

Just as I had done so many years before when I had first read *A Night to Remember*, I did not identify with my actual kinspeople from that time. I would not be going as an 'enterprising Third Class waif'. No, I was going to be a First Class passenger, complete with a magnificent, museum-worthy Victorian vintage black velvet and jet-beaded cape I had been gifted from someone whose relative had once been the wardrobe mistress at the Gate Theatre.

On the evening of the party, all dressed up, I took a taxi across town to Jon's home. 'Nightswimming' by REM was playing on a loop downstairs as guests-stroke-passengers arrived. There was an envelope for each guest. It contained a schedule of the evening's events and a boarding pass. Jon had allocated us each a name of an Irish Third Class passenger; we were to discover at the end of the night if we had survived or not.

The evening's events were timed to coincide in real time with the centenary of the sinking.

10.30 p.m. Welcome from the Captain

11.30 p.m. Iceberg alert

11.40 p.m. Direct hit

11.41 p.m.–02.19 a.m. Heavy drinking

00.00 Jack 'n' Rose prize (best costume)

2.20 a.m. Remembrance for the *Titanic*

2.30 a.m. Lifeboats and legacies – please donate to our RNLI Howth collection

Upstairs, in the 'First Class Saloon', a dinner buffet was laid out. There was not a single woman I can recall dressed as a Third Class passenger, although there was at least one Third Class male passenger in the form of Jack. Someone was wearing a deckchair. Two people bobbed around together, joined like Siamese twins by their costume, which was an astonishingly accurate two-piece handmade model of the *Titanic*, with the addition of Barbie and Ken dolls dressed as Rose and Jack up in the prow.

Jon himself was dressed as Captain Smith, complete with cap and a white costume so shinily acrylic that it would probably have set the house on fire if it had even seen sight of a lit match.

The night passed, punctuated by Jon ringing the 'ship's bell' at intervals to inform us first we had hit the iceberg, then that we were sinking, and finally that it was now everyone for themselves because anyone not in a lifeboat was in the freezing water. At midnight, the duo dressed as the *Titanic* had won the Jack 'n' Rose costume prize. Don't ask me what it was. To use a maritime expression, we were all three sheets to the wind by then. I had abandoned my extraordinarily heavy and hot beaded cape somewhere. Also, my shoes and any remaining principles.

At 2.20 a.m., Jon went down with the ship. I seem to recall he made a speech and temporarily vanished under a table. Then someone started playing the piano, more bottles of wine were opened, more cocktails mixed and the party continued until dawn.

At some point, our drowned captain brought out a board with the names of the Irish Third Class passengers pinned to it and revealed which of them had survived. I cannot now remember the name of the woman that had been written on my piece of paper. I lost my boarding pass in the taxi on the way home.

I texted Jon when writing this essay. 'Wish I could remember what the name on my boarding pass was. I'm pretty sure I drowned.'

He texted back laconically: 'I think, if you survived, you would remember.'

It was years before I found out what had happened to Eugene Daly. By 1983, the year I wrote to the address on the letter in the book I had found, he had already been dead for almost twenty years. His name is now easily found by an internet search; there are many sites that collate *Titanic* information about passengers and crew who were aboard that maiden voyage.

What I most wanted to find out was if the letter and the inscriptions were authentic. My search turned up the same addresses that he had written down in that shaky blue biro. The Athlone address he had inscribed in the back of the book, where he had marked his name on the passenger list, was where he had been living before he set sail. The Galway address on the letter to the unnamed recipient, a house he had originally rented in the 1920s, also matched the records, as borne out by the 1911 census.

Eugene Daly, a mechanic, was twenty-nine when he boarded the *Titanic* at Cobh. He was travelling with a cousin and a friend. On the night of 14 April, he had been asleep in his cabin when the ship hit the iceberg. His cabin was C-23 on F deck and in a location of the ship that was very close to where it had struck the iceberg. Where he was, the impact was so powerful that not only was he woken up, he was almost tossed from his bed. He dressed, putting on his thick overcoat with its astrakhan collar, and went out, unsure what was happening. Eventually, in the commotion, word spread that the ship was taking on water. He went to the cabin his cousin and their friend were sharing and woke them up.

Just getting out from the lower decks where the Third Class passengers were berthed took time. By the time Daly, his cousin and their friend from home reached an upper deck, there was total chaos. He saw the two women into Lifeboat 15 and then got in himself. An officer told him to get out, but he wouldn't. He wanted to survive. Later, he told the *New York Herald*, 'Life was sweet to me and I wanted to save myself.' Daly was forcibly pulled out of Lifeboat 15. By then, the speed with which the ship was sinking was accelerating by the minute.

The earliest first-hand account Eugene Daly gave of this experience was to a passenger on the *Carpathia*, the ship that came to the rescue after altering course. The *Carpathia*, the only ship which rescued anyone from the water, picked up 705 passengers. Along with the crew, passengers aboard the *Carpathia* helped survivors as best they could.

One of them was Frank Blackmarr, a medical doctor from Chicago on holiday. He was twenty-four. A First Class passenger, he offered one of his cabin berths to a survivor. That person was Eugene Daly, unconscious on arrival, still wearing his overcoat. He was carried to Blackmarr's cabin and revived with hot drinks.

The *Carpathia* took almost four days to reach New York. During that time, Frank Blackmarr conducted four interviews with survivors, interviews which he asked each person to sign, along with a note as to which lifeboat they had been in. One of the four was his cabin-mate, Eugene Daly, whom he interviewed three days after being rescued.

This is from the account Daly gave to Blackmarr, starting with what happened after he had been forcibly removed from Lifeboat 15.

I reached a collapsible boat that was fastened to the deck by two rings. It could not be moved. During that brief time that I worked on cutting one of those ropes, the collapsible was crowded with people hanging upon the edges. The *Titanic* gave a lurch downwards and we were in the water up to our hips.

She rose again slightly and I succeeded in cutting the second rope which held her stern. Another lurch threw this boat and myself off and away from the ship into the water. I fell upon one of the oars and fell into a mass of people. Everything I touched seemed to be women's hair. Children crying, women screaming, and their hair in their face. My God, if I could only forget those hands and faces that I touched.

As I looked over my shoulder, as I was still hanging on to this oar, I could see the enormous funnels of the *Titanic* being submerged in the water. These poor people that covered the water were sucked down in those funnels, each of which was 25 feet in diameter, like flies.

I managed to get away and succeeded in reaching the same boat I had tried to set free from the deck of the *Titanic*. I climbed upon this, and with the other men balanced ourselves in water to our hips until we were rescued. People came up beside us and begged to get on this upturned boat. As a matter of saving ourselves, we were obliged to push them off. I don't seem to be able to forget those men, women and children who gradually slid from our raft into the water.

Frank Blackmarr died in 1958. The four signed unofficial accounts, or statements, that he took on board the *Carpathia* were discovered in the attic of a house in Illinois forty years later, in 1998. They were sold that year for $50,000. Before they were sold, a representative from the *Titanic* Historical Society was allowed to transcribe the documents. The *Titanic* Historical Society is still based in Indian Orchard, Massachusetts, at the same address as Walter Lord had given me back in 1983.

In 1917, Eugene Daly married Lilian Caulfield in the US. They had one daughter, Marion, who was born in Galway in 1925. Unsurprisingly, Daly had found the Atlantic passage back to Ireland traumatic. He refused to cross the ocean again by ship and so they remained in Galway. When his wife died in 1961, he flew across the Atlantic to live with his daughter. He died in 1965 and is buried in St Raymond's Cemetery in the Bronx.

His daughter later wrote about the coat with the astrakhan collar which her father had worn that night of the sinking. 'I remember it well. It hung on the back of my bedroom door. Often on a chilly winter's night, my mother would take it down off the hook and throw it over my little bed for an extra warmth. It felt so good, like warm arms around me. We called it the *Titanic*.'

Jon's number is in my phone as Essential Jon, my essential friend. One day in June 2019, I was driving west when my phone rang. Essential Jon's number came up. I put him on speakerphone.

'Hello!' I chirped.

'Where are you?' Jon asked. He sounded odd. Strained.

'Driving. On the motorway. You're on speakerphone.'

'Are you on your own or is there someone with you?'

'I'm on my own,' I said. I didn't like where this conversation was going.

'I need to talk to you. Can you pull off the motorway?'

'Give me a few minutes,' I said. 'I'll call you back.'

As I sped towards the nearest exit I could find on the M7, my brain started to go through all the reasons why Jon might be sounding so uncharacteristically serious and why he might need to talk to me so urgently. I got off the motorway and pulled up on a grassy verge outside a field full of placid cows. I grabbed my phone.

'Jon?' I said, when he answered. 'What's wrong?'

All I could hear was the sound of crying on the other end. I caught my breath. Fuck, whatever this is, it's bad, is what I thought.

'Jon? Talk to me. Please.' I held the phone to my ear and waited.

Eventually, Jon told me that he had been diagnosed with cancer. Prostate cancer. He told me that he had been watching his PSA counts over the last few years and how they had spiked significantly recently. He told me how he had gone for tests, then a biopsy, and how the news had come back and it had not been good.

The cows moved slowly around the field as he talked for close on an hour. Of how frightened he felt. Of his confusion and shock. Of how the diagnosis had upended his life, undone the confident, assured way he went about everything. Of how alone he felt. Of the sensation of panic he felt overwhelming him. It was the first time Jon had ever lost his sense of self with me in all the time I had known him. I listened so carefully that day. I talked back to him with urgency and love. Our roles were reversed. It was my turn to try to wind him back down from the sky where he was a flapping kite threatening to break the string that held him secure, to guide him safely back down to the ground again.

When we were finished talking and had ended the call, I remained sitting for a while in my car. My brain was trying to process Jon's news. I was thinking of all the unfamiliar places his cancer was going to bring him in the coming weeks. I was thinking of that terrible word 'cancer' as one that he was now going to know intimately. I was thinking of the information rabbit hole we were both going to go down in the coming days and weeks, but for the first time we would be trying to understand a story neither of us would ever have wanted to know anything about.

In the weeks that followed, we kept in close touch about his forthcoming treatment. His surgery was scheduled for his birthday, a coincidental date that he embraced as a new beginning. He was to present himself for admission at 6.15 a.m. A few days before he was due to have the operation, he texted.

'R. Will you come over the evening before I go to surgery? We can have dinner locally.'

'Are you sure?' I texted back, very surprised. I had thought he would want to be with family, or to just lie low, or want to spend the time quietly psyching himself up for the following day.

'Yes.'

On the day before his birthday, I left the office early and took the DART out to where Jon lives. He met me at the station and we drove a bit, to Sutton beach, and then parked the car. It was a beautiful summer's evening and we both took off our sandals and left them in the car to walk on the beach. Jon's dog ran ahead of us, barking.

'Are you scared?' I asked at some point, the light around us hazy and blue. The tide was out and the sand ridged and wavy where it had been pushed about by the retreating water.

Yes and no. He had tried to take control of the situation by doing his research, by going down the rabbit holes that, this time, we had investigated separately. He had met his surgeon. He was prepared and knew what was coming. He was going to take a taxi by himself in the morning to the hospital and then various family members were going to be there later and when he came home to convalesce.

Jon was prepared to the extent that he had even written a piece about the diagnosis that he was going to post on social media before he went into surgery. 'The whole point is, I don't yet know how things are going to work out for me,' he said. 'Usually, when you read these things, the person is out the other side. I wanted to capture that time when the outcome is still uncertain. It's what I wanted to read myself when I did my research, but I couldn't find anything from that perspective.'

We walked on. The dog was running in and out of the sea, then tearing up and down the beach, her tail moving like a crazed metronome.

'One of the things that struck me most about this whole process,' Jon said, 'is my consultant telling me that, over the years, sometimes he never sees his patients again.'

I didn't understand. 'What do you mean?'

'They get a diagnosis. A bad one. But then they don't do anything about it. They don't come back for surgery. For whatever reason.'

After walking along the beach and before we went out for dinner, we had a drink on Jon's terrace. In many ways, even with the ever-present undercurrent of awareness of what was to happen the next day, it could have been any evening we'd spent together in the past. Laid-back, chatting and riffing, punctuated with bursts of laughter. The dog went into her kennel and snored. It was an utterly normal evening.

'That's the whole point,' Jon said when I mentioned this to him. 'You're the person I wanted to spend time with this evening. I wanted that calmness.'

I was so surprised I couldn't say anything. I don't think of myself as a default calm person. Do we ever see ourselves as others do? But right then, I was just glad that whatever Jon needed from our long friendship on that landmark evening, I was able to give it to him.

Early the next morning, when Jon was out cold, undergoing surgery, I read his social media post. He wrote about receiving his diagnosis and meditating on mortality.

'One in nine men will be diagnosed with prostate cancer in their lifetime. There is every prospect of a good recovery, though guarantees do not exist in cancer, even if we insist they do in normal life. I have made a considered choice for surgery and there may be complications. Men, if you read up on these, they may make you queasy, frightened or freaked. They did me. Until the acceptance that such things are trivial when measured against saving your own life.'

The piece ended with a plea to the reader to share the personal story with 'men you love and with those who love men', to encourage those men to get checked out.

I thought again that morning about our desire to survive – whether it is to be saved from a sinking ship or a cancer diagnosis, the desire to survive is so innate and profound. In the most superficial of ways, I had experienced this myself, by choosing to go to Jon's party as a First Class passenger, the main cohort of survivors of the disaster, particularly women. Even a century on, I rejected the fate of my kinspeople, most of them doomed as they were by class and a lack of wealth.

I still don't understand what motivated Ida Straus to make the choice she did and probably never will, although I continue to think about it from time to time. Perhaps she didn't really believe that the unsinkable ship would actually sink until it was too late and the water was all around her. The men who had received an unnerving diagnosis from Jon's consultant but who had not come back for treatment, perhaps they, too, had not quite believed what the future held for them until it was too late.

Walter Lord died in 2002. At the time of his death, he was still residing at his Manhattan home from where he had written to me almost two decades earlier. Over the course of his life, he had indeed amassed a remarkable collection of *Titanic* artefacts, many of which had been given to him by survivors whom he had interviewed. Among them was the toy pig that played a tune when its tail was turned and with which Edith Russell had famously entertained a crying baby in Lifeboat 11.

Lord bequeathed the collection to the Maritime Museum in Greenwich, England. As it turns out, the mechanism inside the pig had detached from the tail, which had acted as a crank, and it had long since stopped working. At Greenwich, the pig was X-rayed and the location and type of mechanism was identified. The black-and-white pig itself was made of wood, papier mâché and covered in actual pigskin.

After the team at Greenwich had X-rayed the pig and identified the location of the mechanism, they managed to get it playing by using a small brass rod to gently turn the mechanism inside. They played it just three times and made a recording. Unsure as to what the tune was called, the recording was posted on the internet and the public invited to identify it. 'Maxixe', which is how Lord had described it, is not the actual name of the song but of a genre, a song played to accompany a South American dance.

Within a day, listeners had identified the tune as 'La Sorella (La Mattchiche)' by Charles Borel-Clerc. Composed in 1905, it's a Brazilian tango. You can hear the recording yourself on the internet; it's there for anyone to listen to, accompanied with an image of the toy pig itself.

The tune Edith Russell's pig played in an open boat more than a century ago while hundreds drowned nearby is sweet and tinkly and hesitant. I'm listening to it as I type. I can't get the images of that April night out of my head, the hair of the drowning that Eugene Daly touched as he fought for his own survival. 'Life was sweet to me, and I wanted to save myself.'

In the midst of that terrible night, the tinkly tune of the musical toy pig was the most fragile of sound buffers between the silence of the living and the screams of the dying. That musical toy has now out-survived all who were on board the *Titanic* more than a century ago, and those of us alive in this century can still listen to the haunting tune it played.

As for my essential friend, Jon, he made a full and excellent recovery.

THE JOURNALIST AND THE MURDERER 'FRIENDS'

'Every journalist who is not too stupid or too full of himself to notice what is going on knows that what he does is morally indefensible.'

THIS IS THE startling and famous opening sentence to Janet Malcolm's book *The Journalist and the Murderer*, first published back in 1990. Malcolm is an American-born journalist and writer and this book is, at base, about the ethics of journalism. She makes the analogy that reporters are like old-fashioned tricksters who prey on the vulnerable and vain for the purposes of gaining their trust. Instead of parting them from their money like charlatan salesmen, the journalist's currency is personal stories, the more disturbing and intimate the better. Then the journalist betrays the trust that has been placed in them by stitching their interviewees up when the newspaper story runs.

Her book-length analysis is a bit more subtle than that, but it posits the argument that no matter how well intentioned a reporter is, the relationship between any reporter and their interviewee is unbalanced right from the beginning. No matter how nuanced a connection between the various parties, it's the journalist who holds all the power, because they will always tell the story from their own perspective. As a result, it can only ever be an imperfect version of the other person's story, no matter how ethical a reporter is, let alone one with the flimsiest grasp of ethics.

I never studied journalism but it's what I have made my living at for more than two decades, as a full-time features writer at the *Irish Times*. I learned as I went along. I am still learning. I have to keep reminding myself that when I show up with notebook and recorder, frequently because something traumatic has happened to the interviewee or their wider family, this is usually the first time the interviewee has ever met a journalist. Most ordinary members of the public have never before had the experience of being interviewed.

I get to drink the tea or coffee offered and listen to the story and then I go away and write the story and usually never meet or hear from these people ever again. I'm long gone once the story is published but the people I have talked to have to live with whatever personal or societal consequences occur as a result. I don't consider what I do as 'morally indefensible', but I absolutely understand, as Janet Malcolm points out so bluntly, that the balance of power is eternally skewed in my direction and that of every other working journalist.

All I can do is try to be as empathetic, responsible and ethical as possible and, even so, there are people I have interviewed over the course of two decades who have felt hurt by the experience, or misrepresented, or both. I know there are, because some of them wrote afterwards to tell me so.

The main thing is, I agree with Janet Malcolm: interviewees are definitely not my friends. I am there to murder them, so why would I expect or seek any friendship? And yet, there are some people I have interviewed whom I have never forgotten, some tinder lit during or around the interview experience that remains among the most meaningful of my adult life, fires that still blaze in my memory. It is the most unusual kind of a fleeting interaction, of a brief and powerful kinship, of a recognition that no matter how I use my notebook as armour, sometimes I unexpectedly get struck in the soul when the person unwittingly pierces my professional steel.

The Mullingar Bachelor Festival in 1998. I hadn't been working at the paper long and everything was equally novel and disparate and unexpected. One Friday in late July of that year, I was dispatched to Mullingar, County Westmeath, by my features editor, Caroline Walsh.

It was only when I looked in our archive for the piece I wrote that I remembered the proper name of the festival: the Mullingar – insert brand name of a famous beer here – International Bachelor Competition. It was the first year the event was to be held in a marquee; in previous years, the competition had been held in a local hotel. I took the bus to Mullingar; at the time, I did not drive and sometimes hitchhiked back to Dublin from assignments when public transport times fell unfeasibly late after I had finished the job.

As the event was during the evening, I was staying overnight. The local hotel was booked out with the international bachelors and their many supporters, so I was staying in a B&B in the town. When I booked it over the landline office phone, in the days when you looked in a phone book for numbers and could not avail yourself of TripAdvisor, or indeed the entire internet, I had not realized the said B&B was also a pub.

It was early evening when I arrived. I looked for a reception area but could find none. So I walked into the bar, where six men of varying ages, from middle age to long past retirement age, were at the counter, in a classic pose straight out of a

National Geographic photographer's dream, should they have been wandering around Westmeath back in the 1950s and seeking a classic Irish cliché. Each man had a pint of the famous bachelor-sponsored beer in their hand, each one had a tweed cap, each one had an inebriated face of character. A quivering halo of cigarette smoke hung over each head. They turned as one to stare as I walked in.

'I'm just wondering where check-in is?'

'This is check-in. You check in here at the bar,' a man behind the counter said. 'This is the journalist from Dublin,' he explained to his customers. 'The *Irish Times* and all.' He enunciated the name of the paper with amused derision, in the way you might describe the experience of unexpectedly walking into dogshit while wearing your favourite pair of shoes.

'Very fancy!' one of his customers said. The others guffawed. I wondered if I should say I was not actually from Dublin, I was from Clare, but knew it was pointless.

The barman thumped a key with an orange plastic keyring down on the counter. 'Will you be wanting a shower?'

'Pardon?'

'Will. You. Be. Wanting. A. Shower,' he repeated.

I was taken aback. 'Well, yes.' Didn't everyone want to have a shower when they stayed overnight somewhere?

'Will you be wanting it now, or in the morning?'

The customers had put down their pints and were listening avidly to this exchange about the timetable for my future ablutions.

'Why does it matter?' I managed, mortified at the possible image of my naked self going through the male heads of all in the bar.

'Because if you're having your shower now, I have to put

the bucket out,' the barman said gleefully. 'The shower leaks something terrible. And your room is over the bar, so if you're having it now, I have to get the bucket ready.'

The customers roared. I took the key and fled upstairs, to a room that stank of cigarette smoke. I stayed only long enough to drop my bag. I most definitely did not have a shower. I grabbed my notebook and went in search of the marquee.

The marquee was in a field on the edge of the town and a fairground was set up alongside it. I got there for 8 p.m., as agreed with the PR person in advance, and noted that while I had arrived on foot, some attendees were driving into the field on tractors. This was the final event of the week, during which time the winning bachelor was to be chosen. There was to be a gala dinner for some three hundred people, and I discovered that tables were served seemingly unending free pints of the bachelor-festival-sponsored beer.

The bachelors were to be interviewed on stage after this merry dinner by Maxi, one of the three members of a former band that were big in Ireland in the 1960s and '70s. The other two were Dick and Twink, although none of these three names was their actual first name.

These are extracts from the piece I wrote afterwards.

There's a canopy of smoke over the table where we're sitting and every now and then the door of the dome flaps open beside us to reveal the twinkling lights of the fairground which has been set up in the adjoining field. Children scream. The smell of chips and candyfloss wafts in. Then the door flaps shut again and we're enclosed in the testosterone zone again . . .

Maxi is introduced on stage as 'The little woman with the big name' . . .

Pierre Royer (26) doesn't speak any English, apart from the useful phrase he acquired recently, 'World Cup'. On stage with Pierre is Isabelle Vigouroux, a young Frenchwoman who is working in Mullingar and who is his translator for the evening. The interview is like a three-way long-distance phone call, with gaps in between the questions and answers, but the audience loves it. 'How have you got on with the Irish girls you've met here?' Maxi asks. 'I speak the body language,' Isabelle translates.

Pierre explains that the reason he is still a bachelor is 'because in France you have to be a poet to touch hearts and I am not a poet'. A sigh goes around the dome . . .

Jimmy Cullinane (26) is the Munster Bachelor. 'If you want to meet a girl, you have to act as funny as possible,' he tells Maxi. 'And why wouldn't you just be yourself, Jimmy?' Jimmy looks amazed at this suggestion. 'If I was just myself,' he explains patiently, 'I'd be left sitting in the corner all night and none of the girls would talk to me' . . .

Last up on stage is Pat Connolly (26) from New York. Pat is about ten feet tall, is wearing a black-and-white chequered waistcoat and a huge smile . . .

It's after midnight now and the noise level from the audience has risen gradually over the evening, with people trooping to the bar and swapping seats. But within two minutes of Pat arriving on stage, the place goes quiet. I'm sitting out front now. 'He's got class,' one girl whispers to her companion, who replies something which is unprintable verbatim but which goes along the lines of, 'I'd like to take that nice young man home with me.'

At some point in the evening, I decided to abandon my default strict policy of never drinking on the job. I drank more than one of the free pints of beer on offer and wondered when the elastic night would end. There were ad hoc renditions of 'Molly Malone' by the competing bachelors, who must have been introduced to it during their karaoke sessions earlier that week. The Scottish bachelor asked me to guess what was in his sporran. I wondered how the people who had arrived on tractors were going to get home.

Just when New York Pat was about to play the accordion, which was to be his party piece and the penultimate event before the announcement of the winning bachelor, the lights literally went out. The generator had packed up. It had just turned midnight and, like Cinderella, the generator simply absented itself, unannounced, from the festivities.

Havoc swiftly ensued. In the era before mobile phones, temporary illumination was provided by many cigarette lighters flickering in the darkness. There was roaring and laughing and screeching. The people who had arrived on tractors went outside and moved the tractors so that their headlights now shone into the tent. Other people, still dressed in their tuxes, tried to fix the generator, cursing startlingly loudly all the while.

I was so committed to doing my job, especially being so new to it and so loyal to my brilliant editor, Caroline, that I felt professionally obliged to wait it out to discover who had won. There was no Twitter, Instagram or Facebook back in that Mullingar night to update events in hashtag real time.

And so I stayed sitting there in the almost-dark marquee, a bit drunk, writing illegible notes in the notebook I could no longer see properly, looking at the swirling glimmers from dozens of lighters and listening to people delightedly singing 'New York, New York' in improvised honour of the popular bachelor whose interview had been cut short.

I realized with an epiphanic jolt that I was fantastically happy. So *this* was what being a journalist meant: having unpredictable experiences during the course of reporting, including someone asking when you wanted your shower, and meeting all sorts of people in all sorts of places and never quite knowing how things might turn out.

And that's exactly what I have been discovering ever since, including some unforgettable encounters with people whom I came to murder, but who murdered me instead.

Years ago, I went to do a story on a hospice in Dublin. It was coming up to Christmas time and the piece was to help generate some publicity for their annual fundraising event: sponsoring Christmas lights on a tree. To showcase how some of this money was spent, I was to talk to some of the people who availed themselves of the services the hospice provided.

The hospice had a day centre which offered support and ancillary services on a weekly basis to people who did not yet need to be in full-time hospice care but who would, someday in the future. I talked to resolutely positive and cheerful women at varying stages of cancer who said how much they loved getting their hair and nails done and having massages, and to the kind, attentive people who volunteered on a weekly basis to drive them from home to hospice and back again. Monies from the annual fundraising helped to pay for these life-enhancing activities and for the volunteers' petrol.

The woman who gave me the anchor interview was happy both to go on the record and to be photographed. So I had 'got everything I needed', as the phrase goes, and was gathering up my coat and bag, ready to make my exit, when one of the hospice staff took me aside.

'There is a man here who heard a journalist from the *Irish Times* was coming to do an article, and he wants to talk to you.'

I was surprised by this late and unexpected addition to the interview cohort, but agreed. I always say yes in situations like this. You never know what else people have to say, or what other things might emerge in a story, but most of all, if people want to go out of their way to talk to me, the very least I can do is always listen to what they have to say.

We walked along the calm corridors, making inconsequential talk. I privately meditated on how incredibly kind the staff were, and how cheerful, and how I myself could never, ever work in a hospice. I wondered how this man who wanted to talk to me was availing himself of the additional services that the annual fundraiser provided, and was about to ask just this question when we stopped outside a door that was ajar.

The woman I was with knocked.

'Come in,' responded a faint, but expectant, voice.

The two of us walked into a room where a man lay on a bed, an iPad in his hands. He had turned to look at us and was smiling in welcome. I was introduced, and then the woman I was with left me, closing the door behind her.

It was immediately clear to me that this man smiling up at me was not availing himself of any additional ancillary services. This man, gaunt and hollow as a ghost in the bed, was dying. The most substantial thing about him was the blocky shape of the iPad that was now lying on his chest, as if it was the only thing anchoring him to the bed; that, without its weight, he would simply float away.

I sat down on the chair beside his bed and fretted that I would pass out, so shockingly close as he was to death. He was so sincerely cheerful; telling me that he wanted me to write in my article how very kind and very wonderful the staff were, how happy they had made him and his family in his dying days, and, meanwhile, would I look at this mad expensive new gadget his son had bought for him, this iPad yoke, which was only on loan to him anyway, as he'd be dead soon and the son would have it back. And would I please, please, please be sure not to forget to put in my article how I had met him and how he wanted to acknowledge all that the staff had done for him?

I knew there was no way I was going to be able to use any of these heartfelt wishes in my piece. I also knew that I was very close to crying, to sobbing. Not once have I ever lost it in front of an interviewee, and I hope I never will. Foremost in my mind was that I did not want to distress a dying man by crying in front of him, but I also knew I had to get out of there soon. His startling courage and his gallant determination to publicly credit the people who were helping him to have a peaceful death was undoing me, minute by minute, second by second.

The door opened again. The woman was back. I gently patted the man's fragile hand and said how glad and honoured I was to have met him. We were out in the corridor again and the woman was continuing with the same inconsequential filler talk that I can usually keep going for ever, no problem.

'Excuse me,' I said, cutting across her. 'Can you please show me where the Ladies is?' The words came out in a gulp.

In the Ladies, I locked the stall door and sobbed. I was in there for a while. I felt I had already failed the man who had asked me on his deathbed to do something for him, a vital something that was not about him but about the exceptional care he was receiving in Our Lady's Hospice. Then I washed my hands with vigour, grimly reapplied some make-up and strode out into the corridor again.

'Are you all right?' the woman asked. She looked anxious. 'I'm sorry,' she said. 'We are so used to seeing dying people here we forget that . . .' And then trailed off.

'I'm fine!' I said brightly, digging my nails into my palms and wishing they were much longer and a whole lot sharper. 'Apologies for the delay. Had to take a quick call.'

Saying goodbye at the door, I asked her how long the man had to live.

'No more than a day or two.'

I went straight back to the office and wrote up my story, staying on brief. It was true I was on a tight deadline and word-count and couldn't find a way of changing tone and gears to include the dying man I had met at the end. It was more than that, though: I was still processing the terrible intimacy of what had happened. I filed the story and estimated with grim relief that it would come out after the man had died so he would not know I had betrayed him.

With another decade of experience behind me since then, I know now the obvious story from that day was to write about that man whose dying wishes so poignantly encapsulated everything that was so important about hospice care. In truth, I know I knew it then. I should have found a way to do it: spoken to my editor; explained how the story had changed; emerged from the haze of my shock of having been personally affected to do the job that should have been done. The end result was, I got it wrong, and that troubles me very much.

There is probably not a month that goes by in the decade since that I don't think of that man and the experience of witnessing someone I did not know hover right there on the frontier between life and death. I try not to think of how I failed him. I think instead of his genuine cheerfulness in his acceptance of imminent death and his transparent desire to be kind, to be thoughtful, to think of people other than himself, even at the very end of his life.

In 2011, which, you may note, was not long after the worst economic recession before 2020 came along and changed everything, the village of Two Mile Borris in County Tipperary received some startling news. Well, it was certainly startling to me, but the people I subsequently interviewed there took the nascent development entirely for granted.

In June of that year, a €460 million, 800-acre development was granted planning permission for a site just outside Borris, as it is locally known. The developer was Tipperary-born businessman Richard Quirke.

The unlikely development for this part of rural Ireland was for a casino, an eight-storey, 500-room hotel, an all-weather racecourse and a replica of the White House, the original of which had been designed by Irishman James Hoban. There was also to be a greyhound track, a four-pad heliport, an eighteen-hole golf course and parking for six thousand vehicles. Oh, and a replica of a New England-style wooden chapel, which would host weddings, with the banquets then taking place in the replica White House. Planning permission was refused for an entertainment venue with a retractable roof and an audience capacity of fifteen thousand.

There were to be one thousand jobs created in the running of this vast enterprise, and two thousand in the construction of it. I was dispatched to Tipperary the week the news broke to discover what the locals thought of it all.

It turned out that the locals were as one in supporting the development. Their only complaint was that the venue for fifteen thousand people had been refused planning permission. I wondered aloud how all these tourists were meant to arrive into Two Mile Borris from abroad, as the locals made it clear that they expected the casino, hotel, White House, etc., to be frequented entirely by international tourists.

'Buses. They'll come in on buses,' one person suggested. 'There will be buses to meet them at the airport, I suppose.'

Another told me, 'It'll be very handy for people in Europe who want to go to Las Vegas. They won't have to travel to America at all. They can come to Two Mile Borris instead.'

With the exception of one person I talked to, nobody had ever been in a casino themselves. The one person who was familiar with casinos was a man home on holidays from Australia, a country where there are many large casinos. We were talking in Bannon's Bar, on the main street. He told me that 'because of where this casino is, it's an overnight experience. In my opinion, five hundred rooms is not nearly enough. Five thousand rooms would be more like it for a resort casino.'

At the time, there were exactly no hotel rooms in Two Mile Borris. I knew this, because I was obliged to stay elsewhere in the county while reporting the story.

When I had finished doing my interviews, I decided to go and look at the 800-acre site. I asked for directions: the site was two kilometres away from the village. I had a copy of An Bord Pleanála's summary of the design concept with me. They were in favour of the development. 'The board may consider that the scheme would not detract from, but rather improve and add to, the overall visual amenity of what is now a relatively flat, featureless, unpopulated rural landscape.'

It had started to drizzle by the time I was driving along the road that bisected a relatively flat, featureless, unpopulated rural landscape. I could hear the hum of the motorway not far away. Was I looking at the right place? I wasn't sure. I parked my car and got out to stare at the fields. I have a pretty vivid imagination but, try as I would, I simply could not imagine a vast development of helipads and a casino and a 500-bedroom hotel that apparently was not a tenth large enough to accommodate all the future eager visitors to the Las Vegas of Ireland.

A tractor passed me. Then it stopped and started to reverse back. A man leaned out the window.

'Are ye looking for something?'

I explained what I was doing.

He cut off the engine, jumped down from the tractor and came to stand beside me. It was raining quite hard by then, so he was clearly dedicated to telling me whatever he was about to tell me. 'Now!' he said, and pointed to the field but one opposite from where I was parked. 'Look over there.'

I looked.

'See those trees, and that fence?'

'I do.'

'Now, just around there, that is where the replica White House is going to be! It's going to be mighty, so it will. Our very own White House. Sure, maybe even the President of the US of A himself will come over and stay in it for his holidays!'

He was being completely serious.

I couldn't help it, I just cracked up laughing. It was, flat out, the single most brilliantly surreal experience I have ever had in all my journalism career. Whenever I feel a bit low, I remember that afternoon and the fantastically enthusiastic farmer who stopped to tell me in which part of a field in Tipperary the replica White House would be constructed.

Nothing in the development was ever built.

There is still only one Las Vegas, and it's definitely not in County Tipperary.

Colin, which is not his real name, for reasons that will soon become obvious, was already in the restaurant in Phonsavan when we showed up, us being myself and Brenda, my friend and photographer colleague. It was 2017 and the two of us were in Laos, doing a story on the staggering amount of unexploded ordnance that still lay under the surface of so many of the country's fields. The US dropped an incredible 270 million bombs on Laos during the Vietnam War, a fact that many people still don't know.

On any one day, more than three thousand people are working on clearance of the estimated one third bombs of the total bombs that did not explode – all 90 million of them. The bombs that were dropped more than half a century ago are still exploding – when children find them and think they are playthings; when a farmer digs too deep and strikes one; when someone walking stands on one.

Brenda and I had been out that day with an organization that cleared mines, one of several in the country that worked to clear these vast quantities of unexploded ordnance. We were shadowing them around as they operated metal detectors in open farmland. We watched as they carefully unearthed BLU-26 cluster bomblets, objects which, it was made clear to us, if we stood too close to them, would kill us if they exploded.

Prior to travel, we had been obliged to provide details of

our blood groups, a first for both of us, on any assignment. The drill was, whenever the team arrived at a new location, they first did a test run to the nearest hospital, in case serious injury should occur. That morning, the medical officer had told us functionally that the nearest hospital was forty-five minutes away. 'In case you need a blood transfusion.'

It was a challenging assignment for a number of reasons, not least because we only discovered late in the process that we were obliged to hire a government official to observe us at work. This meant we also had to pay for this government official's flight from Vientiane, the capital, and for her hotel every night, and a daily per diem for her meals. We called her, as one would, 'The Spy', although not, obviously, to her face. She accompanied us everywhere during the day, except to meals, for which I am quite certain both parties were mutually grateful.

However, aside from not being monitored at meals, Brenda and I were even more grateful that The Spy did not come with us to the bars we managed to seek out at the end of long, hot, intense days. In these bars, the two of us tried to debrief, plan for the next day's reporting and decompress after spending time with bomb-damaged survivors and their families. These survivors had been variously horribly maimed and/or blinded by unwittingly stepping on ordnance.

The previous day, I had had to try very hard not to flinch while interviewing (via a translator) a man called Yeyang Yang whose upper torso and much of his face had melted with burns when a bomb went off when he had been scavenging through the local dump. (Brenda, I am proud to relate, was to later win a Press Photographers Association of Ireland Award for her can't-look-away-from-this, necessarily disturbing and also deeply humane portrait of Yeyang Yang, with his little daughter, Syya, who had spontaneously climbed up on to his lap during the shoot.)

Phonsavan was a very small town with one unsurfaced, dusty main street, eye-popping displays of empty bombshells, missiles, rockets and grenades of various sizes outside each establishment. Shells had been turned into makeshift flower planters, or fences; they even formed part of the construction of some of the houses we had seen in rural Laos.

There was not much choice by way of restaurants in Phonsavan and we had found a backpacker place called Craters, in homage to the giant empty bombshells lined up either side of its entrance.

Colin was the only other person in there, one of a number of expats who worked in Laos for various NGOs. He was Australian, sun-walloped, ruddy, tattooed, talkative, a bit hyper, which was unsurprising, given his extremely stressful line of work. He had worked all over the world on different contracts, helping to detonate bombs after warfare, including in Sierra Leone and Iraq.

'G'day!' Colin said, by way of exaggerated Aussie greeting when we arrived in.

The three of us were the only people in the restaurant, a decidedly rustic place, open to the street. Grenades were stuck up on the walls and some had been turned into lights. It was out of tourist season – tourists came to Phonsavan not to see minefields but the nearby arcane Plain of Jars – and Colin was delighted to have some new people to talk to. Or talk at. It was a bit like listening to a radio going in and out of stations.

'When I was looking for a place to rent, there was this fuck-off enormous bomb in the garden. You know the way people have bombs as decorations here? Use them for planters, turn them into tables and benches and fences.' He gestured to the exterior of Craters, with its many upright bombshells. 'Yeah, well, my house came with this bomb, and I could tell it hadn't been detonated and I had to say to the guy who was renting it, "Mate, I can't be renting a place with a fuck-off live bomb in the fucking garden, right?" So he was not happy at all, because it was going to cost him, and he said he had one bigger in his garden and it was absolutely fine, and what was my problem with a live bomb anyway? Most people had one.'

Our food arrived. I watched in astonishment as Colin reached for the plastic bottle of tomato ketchup on the table and squeezed a vast amount of its contents atop his pizza. There was so much ketchup on it when he was finished I couldn't tell what kind of pizza he had ordered.

'Then there was this time I ended up in jail, way back when I had no sense.' He launched into a lively story of illegally held guns in various African states he had worked in and various paramilitary activities in different countries and started eating his ketchup pizza.

'More beer!' he shouted at the waiter, who was less than a metre away. 'Must! Have! More! Beer!'

More beer arrived. Colin remained in a reverie about his gun-possessing days. His overloaded pizza was dripping ketchup all over the table like blood from a stuck pig.

While awaiting the arrival of the pizzas, Brenda had gone out for a cigarette. She'd been gone ages.

Now, suddenly, she ran back inside, waving her phone in one hand and a cigarette in the other.

'Fuck!' she screamed, holding up her phone at me. 'Crazy news!'

I instantly thought another horrendous terrorist event had happened somewhere in the world.

She was struggling to get more words out. 'Coup!' she managed.

'Where? What happened? What country?' I said.

'Coup!' Colin roared with delight. 'I've lived through a few of those! Bloody love coups!'

'Brenda, please tell me what the fuck has happened?' I said.

It emerged that, back in Dublin, in a time zone currently seven hours behind us, the editor of our newspaper had just been secretly ousted by another. We now had a new editor. The announcement of this event had been made a mere half an hour previously in our newsroom, before a stunned and unsuspecting workforce. Without any interview process, or anyone outside a selected few knowing anything about it until it was a fait accompli; a 'coup', indeed, as other media outlets gleefully described it in the coming hours and days.

I don't know about you, but whenever anything seismic happens in my workplace – and this was definitely the most seismic and unprecedented thing that had ever happened re: the editorship in the paper's 160-plus years' history – I immediately think I'm going to get fired. I got made involuntarily redundant – aka fired – from the first proper job I ever had, aged twenty-three, at a publishing company in London and, ever since then, I keep expecting the same thing to happen again.

There was no way to know for sure, as we were 9,500 kilometres away from Dublin, but I thought it best to swiftly err on the side of pessimism by way of preparing for the worst. At the very least, put it this way, it's not good timing to be on the other side of the world reporting on unexploded bombs when your newspaper at home has had an explosive of a different kind put under it.

'I'm going to get fired,' I announced to Colin. 'I've probably been fired already.'

Brenda, who sensibly at no point ever shared any of my pessimism about the future of her own job, was on her phone reading texts from colleagues back in the office. I looked at my phone, which I had turned to silent before coming to the restaurant. There were missed calls and several unread texts. For the next while, the three of us broke off like satellites into our three separate, slightly crazed monologues, periodically apologizing for ignoring each other.

Colin summoned the waiter again. He was now speaking only in words and mangled sentences that ended in exclamation points. 'Another pizza! More beer! Coups! Love a good coup!'

Another pizza arrived for him, and more beers for us all. This time, I saw what was on the pizza before it, too, disappeared under another layer of ketchup. Meat. There was now so much ketchup everywhere it looked as if it was mobile, moving like lava atop the pizza and falling on to the already horribly sticky table.

By now, Colin was in agreement with me that I had lost my job. He decided he was going to cheer me up, on account of having lost my job in a coup, while assuring us that if he had still had his guns and, by the way, he did actually know where to get guns these days, he would just go to Dublin and shoot whoever had fired me, because he wasn't bragging or anything, but he had in fact shot many bullets from many a gun back in the day and some of them had been into people.

Talking about coups somehow provoked Colin's patriotic

side in solidarity with us. He told us he was practically Irish himself, having some distant relative of Irish descent. It was at this point that he started loudly playing rebel Irish songs on his phone, and banging his fists on the table.

'Come out, ye Black and Tans, come out and fight me like a man!'

Now he was on his unsteady feet, marching around the restaurant, singing along to the Wolfe Tones on his phone.

> 'A nation once again!
> A nation once again!
> And Ireland, long a province, be
> A nation once again!'

Now, the waiter came over to tell us he had to close up. In truth, it was definitely time for us all to go home. I would obviously have to start looking for a new job, but not tonight. No, tonight I was going to stagger back to our hotel and pass out. Tomorrow was another day, as Scarlett O'Hara once said.

'How will you get home?' I asked Colin. There were ad hoc taxis on the street outside. We knew he lived some considerable distance out of town, further than one could walk, because he had told us.

'Drive!' he said, pointing to a Land Rover parked across the street.

We pleaded, we cajoled, we offered to pay for his taxi. Was there someone we could pay to drive him home in his own Land Rover? We told him he'd kill himself, or other people, or both. He just ordered a tequila while he waited for us to finish 'yapping', as he laughingly put it. He was amused and baffled by our concern.

'Nothing to worry about!'

In the end, what could we do? We left him to it. We watched him get into the Land Rover, start the engine and begin to pull out.

'Jesus, Colin!' I shouted at him from across the road. 'At least put on your headlights!'

He put on his headlights then and drove off into the Laotian darkness, beeping his horn all the way through Phonsavan's single street.

Colin emailed us both the next morning, at the remarkably early time of five o'clock. I, for one, was definitely not awake at five o'clock that following morning, and I very much doubt Brenda was either. Colin reassured us he had got home safely and thanked us for the company and the most entertaining night he'd had in ages. He added – without any irony I could discern – that he could fix me up with a job in Laos if I was indeed fired.

I did not get fired. I think about that insane night very warmly indeed from time to time, and about Colin, with the unexploded bomb in his garden, and his ketchup pizzas, and his knowledge of real coups, and his ability to shoot a gun, and his terrible, terrible drink-driving habit and wonder if he is still alive. I am happy to confess I suspect that he is.

Some years ago, I wrote a ten-part occasional series for the paper called 'Generations'. The idea was to take a kind of snapshot of society through the decades, from those in their tenth to those in their first. There were five interviews to represent each decade. The oldest person I interviewed was a hundred and three, and the youngest was seven. It was like making a jigsaw: trying to find a group of people in geographically diverse locations and with an even gender balance who were experiencing a wide range of challenges and joys in their lives.

For the first two decades, I worked my own sources to find people: I started with the over-nineties, beginning with the woman of 103. We waited until several upper-decade interviews were 'in the bag', as the unceremonious journalism expression goes, before running the first instalment. My plan for reaching potential interviewees after that was to hope readers would respond to the call-out email at the end of each instalment asking them to nominate either themselves or people they knew for future parts of the series.

People did, indeed, respond; lots of them. My modus operandi at that point was to ask people to email me a short biography of themselves. Then I followed up with a phone call to get more granular detail before making a decision about who to choose, because the longer the series ran, the more emails of recommendation I received. The interviewees also had to be representative in terms of family, some living alone, some married, some living together, some with children, some with none.

And so one day I drove to Kilkenny to interview a man in his sixties who had responded to my call-out. He had lost a son to suicide. I wanted to include him for this reason, to let his particular story of loss represent those many other parents in Ireland who had also experienced the death of a child in this way.

At the house, which was in a rural area, his wife said hello and then left us alone while she drove into Kilkenny to run some errands. There was coffee and biscuits, and I went about setting up my laptop and recorder, all the while giving my spiel about the mechanics of the series and the future arrangements with our photographer, who was arriving on a different date.

Cathal – for Cathal was his name – spoke with such extra-ordinary dignity about the life and death of his late son that I felt a little overawed. He had a quality of something which I am not sure I had ever identified as clearly in anyone else but recognized with certainty as the interview progressed as being that of pure grace.

He spoke about how his son had found living too difficult and that the family took solace in the fact that they absolutely believed he was now at peace after such torturous struggles. 'At one moment my heart can be breaking when I think of him, and in the next I think he is now finally getting the peace that he wanted all along,' Cathal said.

When the interview was over, I accepted another cup of coffee and thanked him for telling me his story; I told him I would try to do it justice.

'I heard you on the radio and knew you would understand,' is what he said, out of nowhere. 'That's why I emailed. I knew I could trust you.'

I was flabbergasted. Sometime previously, I had written in our paper about how my hopes to adopt a child had vanished with the change in Irish law around adoptions from countries outside Ireland. It had generated additional media coverage and I had been on one weekend national radio morning talk show to discuss the subject.

In Kilkenny, Cathal had been listening. He heard some-thing watermarked into the way I talked, some profound grief at a loss, the absence of a child who should have been there. But who was not. I felt like I was sitting with a seer, someone who could see right into my soul. Far from me thinking I had chosen him as an interviewee, the truth was, it was he who had chosen me.

We sat there together in the kitchen for a while, saying nothing: the parent who had lost a child and the person who had longed to be a parent and now never would be. We knew instinctively that we both knew that silence is an invaluable part of any vital conversation. Our shared absences pulsed around us; our lost children greeted each other just then somewhere in a dimension where neither of us could ever go. The clock ticked. We sat. We understood and acknowledged each other's unspeakable grief without saying a word. We sat.

Cathal walked me out to my car. Usually, as in pretty much always, I say goodbye to the people whom I interview in their homes at their front door. There is no need for them to go any further. Not this time. I was inarticulately grateful for his accompaniment out to my car, this shared walk of mutual empathy. When it came time to say goodbye, I had an urge to hug him. I had never hugged an interviewee in my life, although a few had hugged me. We did not hug, and in retrospect I am glad we did not, or I would have started to cry and so, I think, might he.

We shook hands instead and I drove away as he stood there in the driveway, waving and waving and waving.

THE DISAPPEARED FRIEND

IN AUGUST 2008, I went to live in Cambridge, Massachusetts, for ten months. I had been awarded a Nieman Fellowship by the Nieman Foundation for Journalism at Harvard. The foundation was established in 1938, and has awarded fellowships to mid-career journalists ever since. It was open only to male citizens of the US in the beginning. The first US women were included in 1946 and, later, it opened up further to include international citizens of any gender.

Last time I checked, more than 1,500 people from almost 100 countries had participated in the programme: I was the third Irish journalist to receive a Nieman. The fellowships are for journalists working in any area of the media and allow you campus-wide free access to pretty much any classes in Harvard's undergraduate and graduate schools you wish to take. They come with a stipend and many fellowship privileges. The application process is lengthy and the selection process competitive.

The news that I had been offered a place came in an email I accessed via a dial-up computer in the only internet café in Trinidad, Cuba, where ten minutes online cost a staggering $20. I spent close to $60 refreshing the email before I fully took in its contents, let alone be able to reply to it. I have never handed over a bundle of cash with more glee. It was Tuesday, 17 February, 2008.

At Cambridge that academic year, there were twenty-nine of us journalists from around the globe, all gathered in fellowship. It is rare in mid-life to have the opportunity to make a whole new set of friends and even more unlikely and marvellous to have all the time you need to build and establish and celebrate those friendships. But that is what happened to many of us Nieman Fellows that charmed year.

I made very many lifelong friends during my time in Cambridge, but the three I spent most time with were Andrea, Julie and Dorothy. Andrea, like me, was a features writer; she worked for the Cleveland *Plain Dealer* in Ohio. Julie covered the narcotics war and associated gangs for the *Monterey County Herald* in California. Dorothy was a reporter and editorial writer for the *Seattle Post-Intelligencer*, known as the *Seattle P-I*, in Washington. Her byline was D. Parvaz, and we sometimes called her D and sometimes Dorothy and sometimes by an affectionate nickname that she would throttle me over if I revealed it.

I met Andrea first. She admired a sparkly hair clip I was wearing when we all arrived for our first orientation session to the Lippmann House, the home of the Nieman Foundation on campus. We bonded pleasingly that first morning, discovering we each possessed a magpie gene for sparkly jewels and accessories. We were both features writers, but all the shared conversations about our various jobs would come later. What mattered initially was that we shared a trivial, but important, aesthetic.

That same morning, a striking-looking woman with short black hair marched over to us both, wearing towering flame-red platform sandals. She stood in front of Andrea, who smiled expectantly.

'Hello! I'm Andrea.'

'You have lipstick on your teeth,' the woman informed her coolly, then marched away.

Andrea and I looked at each other.

'Have I really got lipstick on my teeth?' she whimpered.

'Who is that bitch?' I said.

That bitch turned out to be Dorothy. We never saw the red platforms again; all she ever wore the rest of that Nieman year was black. The red shoes were a one-off anomaly. Afterwards, whenever we teased Dorothy about the lipstick incident, she maintained she had just been trying to help out. 'I thought you'd want to know,' she insisted. 'I thought I was doing a good-citizen act.'

'Dorothy!' one of us would always reply. 'There are ways of saying things!'

That evening, at a party to meet staff and other fellows, we met Julie. Later, writing in the *Monterey County Herald*, Julie described how we four had originally met.

Dorothy is part of a cadre of four who bonded immediately during our Nieman Journalism Fellowship at Harvard in 2008 . . . The night of our first fellowship event in Cambridge, the four of us found a box of free hangers on a curb. Not those icky wire dry-cleaner hangers but the smooth plastic ones that don't tangle in your closet.

And since we're all into clothes, we grabbed them. OK, the other three are the fashionistas – I'm the Quakerly den mom of the group, but I still like clothes. (And thanks to Dorothy's advice, I now wear black eyeliner at least once a week.)

We stuffed our bags and coats and walked into the night with hangers bulging. After that, we were forever known as the Hanger Sisters.

What Julie didn't write is that Dorothy did not take any of the hangers. Years before the Covid-19 pandemic, she was a straight-up germaphobe who used hand sanitizer before each meal. She was appalled at the sight of the three of us gleefully foraging in the box for as many hangers as we could carry. It was tradition in Cambridge at the start of the academic year for people to recycle by putting out unwanted furniture, kitchen items and other household stuff on the sidewalks outside their homes, there for the taking by anyone who wanted them, like the large box of hangers.

'You don't know where those things have been,' Dorothy warned us darkly as we picked through the box.

'In someone's wardrobe, probably? Where those things usually are?' Julie offered, and we fell about laughing.

After the hanger raid, the four of us walked towards the West Side cocktail bar on Massachusetts Avenue. It was beside Huron Cleaners, which had a red neon sign of a clothes hanger in its window and which we saluted with our own newly liberated hangers. At the West Side, which was the first time the four of us sat down together, we talked for hours and hours and raised our Martini glasses joyfully in agreement when Julie christened our quartet the Hanger Sisters.

We became so close so quickly that there was hardly a day that year when we didn't see each other. We were either in class together, or at an event or workshop, or eating together, or in a bar, or just hanging out, always endlessly talking. We had lifetimes to catch up on. We never stopped talking. Sometimes, we skipped events – international speakers with headline names that we really should have gone to – because we just wanted to talk to each other instead.

One evening, about three weeks after arriving in Cambridge,

I was at home in my apartment on Langdon Street. I had not yet cooked dinner in my new home and thought I should do so that night. My phone rang. It was Andrea.

'Where are you?'

'At home.'

She was incredulous. 'What are you doing at home?'

'I'm going to cook dinner.'

'By yourself! Why do you want to be by yourself when you could be with us? What is *wrong* with you?' Andrea was, and is, frequently entertainingly over the top in her declamations, always rending her garments and sticking daggers in her heart. She kept on in this astonished what-is-wrong-with-you strain while I looked around the little kitchen and decided I did not want, after all, to have dinner by myself. I had a partner at the time, but he would not be arriving from Canada for another couple of months. There would be many more times in the future to have dinner alone. Meanwhile, I wanted to make the most of this fellowship year and spend as much time as possible with my new friends.

'Where are you?' I said, reaching for my bag.

After that, I hardly ever even had breakfast at home. On the rare days we did not see each other, we talked at length on the phone. When Dorothy became ill with a horrible migraine, it was Andrea who went with her to a doctor. When Julie was trying to decide on a dress to wear to Obama's inauguration ball in Washington, it was us who chose it for her. (She had the nerve to tell us later she didn't like our choice, but we know we were right.) When Andrea called her beloved Uncle Nick, now dead and whom I was never to meet, she always passed the phone to me so he could talk to this new friend of his niece. When I had a deeply traumatic personal experience midway through the year, it was my Hanger Sisters who circled me protectively and let me cry all I needed to.

Lest this all sounds like something from a Disney movie, let me tell you, we had our moments. Rows big and small, all usually over extremely stupid things. Actually, all of them over extremely stupid things, because I cannot now remember the source of a single one of these rows. Words. Very bad words. Fallings-out. Walking off in steely huffs. Phoning one sister privately to vent about another sister's temporary crimes. We squashed all the normal tests of a lifetime of close female friendship into less than a year.

In the end, no matter how exercised or infuriated or impatient we got with each other, friendship always prevailed. Without ever actually discussing it, we all decided we did not want to waste our precious time together rowing about things that would not matter in a couple of weeks, let alone years from now. We knew our fellowship year was going to be the only time in our lives we would all live within a kilometre of each other and we were going to maximize that opportunity all we could.

Dorothy was the most international of us. She had been born in Isfahan in Iran, to an Iranian father and an American mother. She had lived in Iran until the age of twelve and still spoke Farsi. She held three citizenships: Iranian, Canadian and American. Dorothy particularly cherished her Iranian roots. As a consequence, she was frequently seeking out the best places to eat Persian food around Cambridge and coaxing us to go with her to these restaurants and shisha cafés. We three barbarians accompanied her to these special places of her culture with a marked degree of reluctance and extremely poor grace, due to the important fact that none of these establishments served alcohol.

Dorothy had a ferocious intelligence, a coal-black sense of humour and opinions so strong they could sometimes all but staple-gun some unlucky person to the wall. From behind a lattice of fingers held over my face, I watched her make virtual mincemeat out of people she thought were behaving badly, making stupid comments or just being plain rude. To be honest, if she wasn't my friend, she would intimidate the hell out of me.

We soon discovered that she detested having her photograph taken.

'What are you doing?' she barked to a hapless fellow fellow aiming his new camera in her direction. He had bought it especially to document this unusual year.

'Taking a picture,' he replied, looking baffled to be asked to explain the obvious.

'Did you ask my permission?'

'Dorothy. Can-I-Take-Your-Photo?' he enunciated cheerfully, lifting the camera again and refocusing the lens.

'No. You cannot. Please do not take my picture.'

He made the mistake of thinking she was joking and took a photograph. He did this more than once during that day, when we were all gathered together. I won't repeat the words that were used when the message was finally communicated to the guilty party, but I can report that civil relations between the two of them never recovered.

At the end of that year, we made a yearbook of our time in Cambridge which included a page of photographs for each of us. Dorothy's page had no photographs on it; she was represented simply by a giant typographical D. I guess that tells you how strongly she had made her opinions felt during the year about having her picture taken.

Dorothy did not do pictures, and neither did she do hugs. 'Hugging without ever touching,' was her mantra. That was a new one on the three of us, who unselfconsciously hugged each other on departure and usually on meeting as well, no matter how often in a day we met.

Of the four of us, it was Dorothy who never expressed a single doubt about why she had been awarded a Nieman Fellowship. Andrea, Julie and I kept repeating that we would soon be found out as frauds and frogmarched off to the airport to be packed back home in disgrace. We were only half joking. For a shamefully long time that year, the three of us freely admitted to not believing that our prior work as reporters and our individual characters, ideas and motivations had the merit such a prestigious fellowship acknowledged.

It was notable in our class that it was mostly women who could hardly believe they had had the talent to be awarded a journalism fellowship; in general, the men had no trouble at all accepting their success as some inevitable due. However, Dorothy lacked no confidence in that regard. I first admired her for it and then made a conscious decision to be more like her and start believing in myself as a journalist a bit more.

Halfway through the year, Dorothy's paper, the Hearst-owned *Seattle P-I*, announced out of nowhere that unless they could find a buyer, the paper would close in six weeks. Dorothy heard the news when she was visiting her then boyfriend in London at Christmas. Andrea and I went to Logan Airport to meet her off the plane on the snowy January evening when she returned; Julie had not yet come back from California after Christmas. Dorothy was still stunned by the news.

'I'm going to be out of a job,' she said flatly, picking at the cheese board in the Cambridge restaurant we brought her to.

We had hoped cheese, possibly Dorothy's favourite thing to eat, might help, but cheese, oddly enough, does not mend all ills, let alone the disaster of your employer about to go out of business. 'Who would possibly buy a paper in 2009?'

For once, Andrea and I did not know what to say. We both knew that the prospect of anyone coming forward to buy a newspaper in an era where American newspapers were closing their Washington bureaus was zero. There were other fellows in our class who were being offered buy-outs as their papers sought to cut costs. The one question everyone was asking back then was what was 'the future of the media'. They are still asking it now.

The *Seattle P-I* duly closed after the token notice time of six weeks. It migrated online, with a skeleton staff. Dorothy was offered a job there at a much-reduced salary. She turned it down and an inevitable gloom settled over the rest of her fellowship year; the worry of what to do next and where to go after we all left in the summer was omnipresent. We three other Hanger Sisters rent our garments in shared sympathy and tried our best to keep our newly unemployed sister cheerful.

Leaving Cambridge in June 2009 was as bad as you might think it would be after ten months' freedom from work, a generous monthly stipend to live on and the riches of Harvard's campus laid open to us. Dorothy left first, then me. Andrea and Julie came to Logan Airport to see me off. Before I got on the plane to Ireland, I went into the Ladies and sobbed. My phone buzzed constantly in my bag with messages from the Nieman sisters and fellow fellows I had just left behind. I realized how much I loved each of my Hanger Sisters, what extraordinary friends those three women had become to me and how utterly different each of them was. I sobbed some more as I read these farewell messages that kept beeping on my phone while I stood between the washbasins and the hand dryers, which kept going off like sirens every time I moved too close to them.

In the years that followed, many of us from the fellowship kept in touch and, of course, we four sisters did. We visited each other, and emailed and called, and managed several reunions, both with the wider class and with each other. Whenever we met, we took up where we had left off and were at once again back in the easy sisterhood of our Nieman year. Andrea, Julie and I had returned to our various newspapers. Dorothy got a job with Al Jazeera and moved to Doha, Qatar.

In May 2011, the entire Hanger Sisterhood were due to meet in Cambridge for a long weekend to mark the retirement of the director of the foundation, Bob Giles, or its 'curator', as the pleasingly archaic term was. Many of our class were to be there, along with class members from other years when Bob had been curator. We Hanger Sisters had been exchanging emails about our arrival times and calculating how many of our beloved haunts we could revisit in the time we had.

Our Nieman class, like every other class, had its own private email forum, which we intermittently corresponded on, sharing news and job openings. Monday, 2 May 2011 was a bank holiday in Ireland and I had been out and about, not looking at email. Sometime between getting home and considering making dinner, I looked at our shared email forum and was surprised to see there were several mails from various classmates, all sent that day; it was unusual to have so much activity in a single day.

Then I registered the subject line: 'Dorothy Missing in Syria'.
In disbelief, I opened my email. The first message was
from a classmate who was then bureau chief for the McClatchy
newspaper group in Cairo. She had been the first to see a story
Al Jazeera had posted earlier that day, a story she linked to and
which I read with growing horror.

> Al Jazeera has demanded immediate information from Syria
> about one of its journalists who has been missing in the country
> since Friday afternoon. Dorothy Parvaz left Doha, Qatar, to
> Syria on Friday to help cover events currently taking place in
> the country. However, there has been no contact with the 39-
> year-old since she disembarked from a Qatar Airways flight in
> Damascus . . .
>
> An Al Jazeera spokesman said: 'We are concerned for Doro-
> thy's safety and wellbeing. We are requesting full co-operation
> from the Syrian authorities to determine how she was processed
> at the airport and what her current location is. We want her
> returned to us immediately.'

Our classmate wrote from Cairo: 'I assume she's being
held for questioning somewhere, but the fact that nobody has
heard from her in several days is extremely worrying. Please let
me know if you have ideas on helping find info as to her
whereabouts . . . Perhaps just posting the news story about her
disappearance and spreading awareness is good at this point?'

At least fifteen others had replied to the email thread by
the time I first looked at it.

'Has anyone contacted CPJ [Committee to Protect Jour-
nalists] and Reporters Without Borders?' This was our Mexican
fellow.

It went on and on. Offers to contact influential people and organizations. Suggestions as to who might help. Expressions of shock. Links to a Facebook page that had already been created to Free Dorothy Parvaz.

There was more: a statement from Dorothy's family that had been released to the media at the same time as Al Jazeera had gone public with the story. We had met Dorothy's father, stepmother and sister when they came to visit in Cambridge, and her then boyfriend in London.

'Dorothy Parvaz is a dearly loved daughter, sister and fiancée. We haven't heard from her in four days and believe that she is being held by the Syrian government. Dorothy is a global citizen – she grew up in Iran, UAE, Canada and the United States. We need to know where she is. We need to know who is holding her and that she is comfortable. We need to know that she is safe.'

I sat on my sofa in Dublin and realized I was trembling. My friend had been disappeared. She had already been missing for more than three days. It was more information than I could process.

I had not even known Dorothy was going to Syria to report; she had only just come back to Doha from a long stint covering the recent tsunami in Japan. I had had an email from her the previous Thursday, the day before she had travelled to Syria, a country in an extremely volatile state, where its citizens were protesting the forty-one-year rule of President Bashar al-Assad and his family. Dorothy had not mentioned her imminent trip to Syria in her email to me. Instead, she had written that she would do her best to fight off jet lag so we could all start our Cambridge reunion immediately and there had been an arrangement about where and when to meet.

I went back to my phone. The emails were frantically piling up, Dorothy's name in every subject line. A thought struck me. I turned on the television. My friend was everywhere, her photograph and the news of her disappearance on every news bulletin. Sky News. BBC. Channel 4. All the wire services were carrying the story. I checked the *Irish Times*. My own paper was now running the Reuters wire coverage. The *New York Times* had the story up. So too did the *Washington Post* and the *Guardian*. I looked at Twitter on my phone. Her name was already trending in North America. By that point, I was on the floor, crying.

I called Andrea in Cleveland. We wept down the phone to each other, frantic with worry, neither of us wanting to end the call. Then I called Julie. This was years before Zoom. We were unable to all be on the same call together at the same time; we were splintered in our separate households and cities, able to connect with only one person at a time. We could not unite virtually in our fear and shock.

It is a terrifying and deeply surreal feeling to experience a friend go missing. It's additionally profoundly bizarre to see that friend also become an international story. As journalists, we report dispassionately on the news but, suddenly, it was now my friend, my Hanger Sister, who had become the story, who was making news. It was Alice through the looking glass. It was not the way it was meant to be. It was all wrong.

In the disorientating days that followed, I spent much of my time online. On Wednesday, 4 May, two days after the news broke, Al Jazeera issued a statement to say Syrian officials had contacted them to confirm Dorothy was 'being detained'. There were no further details.

Around the world, my fellow Nieman classmates did what

we could: we wrote and broadcast stories for our various media organizations about Dorothy's disappearance, trying to keep her in the spotlight. I wrote a piece myself for our Saturday paper, sitting in my car by the side of a road in rural Donegal, where I had been sent to cover a spate of ongoing forest fires by arson.

'My friend Dorothy Parvaz is missing. Of all the thousands of words I've written as a journalist over many years, these are the six I can hardly believe I am typing. They feel fictional. They feel wrong. And they are words I wish I never had to see published . . .' it began. I wrote it in under half an hour, the words tumbling out. By the time it ran, on 7 May, she had been missing for nine days.

The BBC World Service picked up the piece, brought me into the studio on 9 May and got me to read out the article, to be broadcast to their international listenership in tandem with an appeal for her release. As I read out the article, I kept simultaneously wondering if Dorothy might just possibly hear it when it was broadcast.

Andrea, Julie and I tried to find humour where we could. There was one particular file picture of Dorothy, an old photograph from her time at the *Seattle P-I.* which ran with most of the stories published and broadcast about her. It managed the impossible: our beautiful friend looked both unrecognizable and a bit sinister. We called it her 'Wanted' photo.

Looking back at my emails from that time, I have no idea how I got up and went to work every day; I was wholly preoccupied by my missing friend. By then, a global campaign, based in Vancouver, to find and free Dorothy was underway. Team Dorothy was led by Kim, herself a journalist, and the sister of D's then boyfriend. I had met her briefly in London at Dorothy's apartment, when Kim was finishing a foreign-correspondent stint in Pakistan and was stopping over en route back to the US. At some point during those days, Kim got in touch with me. The campaign needed someone in Europe to help out with diplomatic and human rights contacts there. I agreed, grateful to have a task. We still did not know for sure where in Syria Dorothy was. I just kept steadfastly hoping she was being held in a room somewhere in the airport in Damascus, a nice, bland room where perhaps there was a conference table and chairs and a whiteboard, and that she was sleeping on the couch there, in that nice, bland, clean, anonymous room.

On Wednesday, 11 May, I flew to Boston for our long-arranged class reunion. I was in a daze. At Logan, I waited for Andrea's flight to get in. She spotted me first and came bounding forwards.

'Oh, sister,' Andrea said, dropping her roughly twenty-five bags, scarves, sunglasses, phones, newspapers, books and magazines as she hugged me. I helped her retrieve the scattered belongings. Andrea was infamous for losing things. One of our nicknames for her was 'Where's My?', because she uttered this expression, followed by the name of some missing object, roughly a hundred times a day. The other, if I may, was 'Lightning', because she was almost always late for everything. Blame Dorothy for that one.

'The fuck, Andrea,' I said, when we were sitting in Legal Seafoods at Logan drinking Bloody Marys and waiting for Julie to get in. 'This whole thing is just batshit crazy.' I had been updating her on the work Kim and everyone else had been doing for D's campaign. In another world and time dimension, all four of us were meant to be meeting up together in Cambridge later that day. We had had it all planned out:

where we would go together and what we would do. I stared around me at the people hurrying past the open-plan restaurant we were sitting in with its cheesy slogan we'd laughed at so often in the past – 'If it isn't fresh, it isn't Legal!' – and wondered for a second if I was in fact dreaming.

Andrea's phone rang. It was Julie. Her flight had landed early. We paid up and rushed to meet her at the baggage carousel. 'Hey, Hangers!' she called to us, waving madly, as we descended on her for a group hug, before decanting into a taxi to Cambridge. For a while, as we chattered in the taxi, talking over each other, as was our wont, and laughing non-stop, everything almost seemed normal, even though nothing was normal.

Julie was staying with another friend and Andrea and I were both sharing a room in the Irving House guest house. The formal events planned for the class reunion and tributes to our retiring curator were to begin on the Friday, although several of us had organized our own gatherings in advance of that.

On the Wednesday night, I found it almost impossible to get to sleep. It wasn't jet lag. It was the constant worry and dread that were at the back of my mind all through that time about Dorothy's safety. We all knew journalists had been killed simply for doing their job. One of our own classmates, Alfredo, who was Mexican, covered the brutal drug war in Mexico for the *Dallas Morning News*. He had taken up his fellowship to temporarily go off the beat after a death threat was delivered to him, a threat that his editor at the *Morning News* had encouraged him to take extremely seriously.

Another classmate, Fatima, had been a friend of the murdered Russian journalist, Anna Politkovskaya. Fatima, who was from Nalchik, the capital of the Kabardino-Balkarian Republic, had herself come to the US on refugee status: she had been given shelter in the US after two unsuccessful attempts on her life, one by being savagely beaten up, and then by poisoning. She had been doing dangerous investigative reporting in the North Caucasus regions, reporting that did not reflect well on Vladimir Putin and his government.

Near dawn, I opened my laptop. I had found a way to contact a high-profile person heading up an international human rights organization, someone Kim had specifically asked me to try to get to. I had been waiting for a final email to put me in contact with this person and it was this email I was now looking for, hoping it had come in overnight.

The email had arrived. So, too, had a confidential one from Kim, to the team of us around the world now working on D's campaign. There was new information.

'Syria says they deported Dorothy on May 1,' she wrote. Deported to Iran. Shit. Shit. Shit. But how? How had she been taken there? Overland? D had, then, been sent to Iran the day before news broke internationally of her disappearance, when we all thought she was still in Damascus somewhere.

'We have not been able to locate Dorothy in Iran. No one knows who has her. My suspicion is she's with the Iranian authorities, in Evin Prison.'

Deep in my consciousness, I had known my optimistic belief that Dorothy was holed up in some nice, bland, clean conference room at Damascus airport was utter fallacy. I googled Evin Prison with trepidation. I had never heard of it before. The Wikipedia entry came up first.

Evin Prison has been accused of committing 'serious human rights abuses' against its political dissidents and critics of the government.

The grounds of the prison include an execution yard, a courtroom and separate blocks for common criminals and female inmates. It was originally operated by the Shah's security and intelligence service.

An execution yard? Had I read that correctly? I had. There was more, much more, in the Wikipedia entry, accounts of the fates of those who had previously been imprisoned there.

On 23 June 2003, Iranian-Canadian photojournalist Zahra Kazemi was arrested for taking photographs in front of the prison and died of blunt trauma to the head while imprisoned. The Iranian government said that she died from a stroke while being interrogated. Doctors examining Kazemi's body found evidence of rape, torture and a skull fracture . . .

I gasped with horror. I kept desperately googling, even though I knew I shouldn't, the way you do when you go down a rabbit hole on the internet with something medical you initially thought was incredibly minor but then, once you start, all sorts of terrifying things come up.

Evin Prison, where inmates are raped, electrocuted and executed . . .

Evin Prison, where women are often kept in solitary confinement. The prisoner can find herself being dragged from her cell on a daily basis to be interrogated, where torture is often applied . . .

Evin Prison, where former inmates have described being subjected to mock executions, beatings and psychological torture . . .

I couldn't believe what I was reading. My eyeballs felt scorched. My head felt as if it was exploding. I couldn't bear it. Our friend, who was so fastidious about hygiene that she used hand sanitizer every time before she ate and who would not take perfectly fine clothes hangers out of a box on the street, what were they doing to her in this hellhole and how could she survive? Was she being raped? Were they torturing her? What could her mental state possibly be now? Even if we could rescue her, was she already so psychologically damaged from the experience that she would never recover?

Once, when I was driving from Dublin to Sligo to stay with friends, I reached a stretch of dual carriageway and, a couple of kilometres in, saw something moving in the distance, on the right. Was it a rabbit? I wondered. My car got closer and the moving thing got bigger. It was not a rabbit. It was a small, lost, brown pet dog with a collar around its neck, owner's disc flying, frantically running along the dual carriageway, so very, very far from home.

I drew alongside. The exhausted dog looked up at me in that splintered second, running as uselessly as a hamster on a hamster wheel. There was a concrete barrier in the median of the dual carriageway and no way to exit. The dog was in a place on a public dual carriageway where no pet should ever be. I realized two things simultaneously: that the dog was not going to be able to escape to safety and that I could not safely stop to rescue it. It would be too dangerous for me and all the other motorists coming behind me.

Knowing all this, I had to keep driving, even though I knew what was going to inevitably happen. The lost dog was going to be struck and killed by a car; when I looked in my wing mirror, I could already see a car swerving to avoid it.

That's what I felt like, that morning in Cambridge, reading about Evin Prison and knowing Dorothy was in there. I felt those same emotions of dread and grief and utter helplessness as I had with the lost dog, but amplified a multitude.

My sobbing woke up Andrea. She came to sit on my bed with me. I showed her Kim's email. I was wailing at this point. I felt absolutely anguished, that Victorian word, as if I was losing my mind, as if I was in some kind of fugue state. My vivid imagination had taken me right inside Evin and there was nowhere it wasn't continuing to go.

'Dorothy is tough,' Andrea said eventually, hugging me tight and trying her best to console us both. 'Much tougher than we think. You have to believe that.'

That lowest day of all the days since Dorothy had gone missing was also the one in which we all laughed, really laughed, for the first time since the news had broken. Kael, a classmate who was a photographer and documentary-maker based in Texas, had not been able to make it to Cambridge. She sent our class an email that day with a photograph attached.

'I thought you'd all get a kick out of this. Dorothy's photo on an e-billboard in Times Square.' Kael had seen it on Facebook, posted by Unity Journalists of Color, an alliance of four American journalism organizations, which had paid to put it there. There was a giant photograph of Dorothy three storeys high on a building, with her name and an appeal for her release. 'She's sure going to love that,' Kael wrote laconically.

The three of us were having lunch when Kael's email came in.

'Dorothy's photo . . .'

'Is in Times Square in New York . . .'

'On a *billboard* . . .'

'If you hate your photo being taken, where is the most unlikely place for it to ever end up?'

'Only the most famous public place in any city in the entire world . . .'

'Oh my *God*, this is fucking fantastic.'

We howled. Oh, we howled like wolves.

By the Friday, 13 May, it was public knowledge that Dorothy was in Iran but not where she was or who was holding her. Al Jazeera put out the story, again demanding that their journalist be freed. By then, Kim had told me that Dorothy was definitely in Evin Prison. Her phone had been turned on for a couple of seconds and those few seconds had been enough time for someone working on the campaign to geo-locate the phone to Evin in Tehran.

Over those few days, I learned more than I ever wanted to know about international diplomacy. Dorothy was a citizen of Iran, the US and Canada, but the Iranian government recognizes Iranian citizenship only when a person with multiple citizenships is in Iran. Vague as I was about geopolitics, even I knew that international relations between Iran and the US were poor. Although, behind the scenes, the US government was doing what it could, it could not become publicly involved as then the situation would become potentially politically extremely dangerous – it would become about two countries in an international disagreement rather than about one missing journalist.

Those days were among the strangest of my life. One moment, Julie, Andrea and I were making black jokes about Dorothy being 'in the clink'. The next I was reading emails about strategy from Kim, who was managing a large team of people, and gleaning how immense the effort was in so many high-level quarters in so many countries to get Dorothy released. The next I was in a bar with a Martini, desperately trying to get images of torture and rape out of my head.

I arranged to meet someone I had known from my Nieman year in Paloma café, off Harvard Square. This person was not someone I had liked much, but he had connections via the Kennedy School of Government with people Kim thought might be able to help us. After our conversation, when I had got the phone numbers and email addresses I needed, he tipped a sachet of sugar into his coffee and stirred it in.

'Do you really think she's still alive?' he tossed out casually.

I was totally blindsided by this comment. Or question. Or whatever completely tactless garbage was coming out of his mouth. I had had several coffees in Paloma in the past. Not for one second did I ever think I would one day be sitting here, listening to someone wonder out loud if a disappeared friend of mine was dead or not. In my inner contempt at his impolitic comment, I also realized with a sudden jolt that he did, in fact, himself believe that Dorothy was now dead.

'Yes. I do. If she were dead, we would have heard by now,' I said, feeling a sensation of vertigo as I uttered the words, even though I was sitting down. I could not get away fast enough after that. I have never seen him since.

On the Monday evening, our last full day together, Andrea, Julie and I made a pilgrimage to the West Side cocktail bar on

Mass Ave where the four of us had first convened. Huron Cleaners was still there, its little red neon hanger sign still glowing in the window.

At West Side, we lifted our glasses.

'To Dorothy! In the clink!'

'To the next time we're all having cocktails together!'

'To the Hanger Sisters!'

On the plane back to Dublin on Tuesday, I felt desolate with loneliness. Nobody in Ireland really understood what I was going through; most people knew nothing at all about the year I'd had in Cambridge. My sister, who had come out to visit for a few days and who had been my sole visitor from Ireland that fellowship year, was the one person in Ireland who had even met all three Hanger Sisters. As the miles between myself and Andrea and Julie increased, I felt more and more isolated and despairing. By then, Dorothy had been missing for eighteen days. Back home in Dublin, I fell into bed, sad and wrecked.

I awoke sometime on Wednesday, 18 May to discover my phone was exploding with text messages and emails and voicemails from our Nieman class.

'Dorothy is free!!!!!!'

'Wake up! D is free!'

'Mimosas for breakfast in Dallas! You're all welcome!'

'D! How weird is it to see everyone talk about you like you're not in the room??!!'

'Hallelujah!'

I scrolled through my phone, frantically looking for an email from Kim. Hard-wired as a reporter to seek facts, unless I saw something official, I wasn't going to allow myself to believe the news. But there it was: confirmation. Kim had sent everyone working on the campaign a statement from D's family. They had just received a call from her in Doha.

'She is safe in Doha and will be coming to Vancouver soon. We can't wait to see her. She said that she was treated well in Iran. She sounded positive and grateful for the support – but a little embarrassed.'

It *was* true. Dorothy was free. She was safe. I was simultaneously exhilarated and also selfishly raging that this news had not come one day earlier, when Andrea, Julie and I were all still in Cambridge and could have celebrated together. Unsurprisingly, when we checked in with each other that day, all of us had had the exact same response to the news.

Dorothy being Dorothy, as soon as she was back in Doha, she went straight to work. I mean pretty much as soon as she got back from the airport. She did a TV interview for Al Jazeera that promptly went around the world and ran on news bulletins all that day and the next. I watched the whole thing back on YouTube. She looked a bit strained. As one would, having been through such an experience. But definitely herself. Wearing black, as usual. And so composed!

This is some of what Dorothy said in her interview. Be warned, it's grim, so if you want to skip this bit, turn the page.

'The beatings I heard almost around the clock were savage,' she said, grimly relating her time in the Syrian secret prison.

'That must have been one of the most scary things,' the interviewer said. 'Hearing what was going on around you and not knowing what was going to happen to you.' No shit, Sherlock, I thought.

'The first night I was there, they took me out, blindfolded and handcuffed, to a courtyard, I am fairly sure for that purpose: to scare me. I heard two separate interrogations and beatings . . .'

'Did they give you any reason as to why you were being held? Is it because you were a journalist?'

'Initially, at the airport, the impression I was given was that [they thought] I might be a US spy for Israel. Then it became quite clear that the fact I worked for Al Jazeera was a huge problem. They equated Al Jazeera with Human Rights Watch for causing problems for them is how it was put to me by my interrogator.'

'Were you aware of the huge media coverage surrounding your disappearance and efforts to find out where you were?'

'No. No, I had no idea,' she said, and went on to explain how she had been taken from Syria to Iran.

'I was in Syria for three days and I was rather forcefully extradited to Iran by three men dragging me on to a plane, kicking and screaming. They told me I was being returned to Qatar. But they misinformed me. ['Misinformed?' I laughed. It was such a typical Dorothy black understatement.] So I arrived in Iran and the Iranian government had to follow through the process of dealing with someone they were told was a spy.'

Shortly after she had finished her Al Jazeera interview, D emailed us, both to our class and separately. She was back in her apartment in Doha, making plans to fly to Vancouver to see her family. She was staggered, incoherently grateful and embarrassed at all we had done for her. 'Your friend lives to see another day and I can't wait to see your smiling faces and to thank you in person soon,' she concluded. 'Lives to see another day' had never had such a literal meaning for any of us.

To me, she wrote, among much else: 'I managed some days okay. Others, I was crushed – a heap of dust on my cell floor.' From her prison cell, she had been thinking of us in Cambridge without her. 'For what it's worth, I agonized over ruining the Nieman reunion. I really did. Even though I place the blame squarely on the Syrians, I still felt awful. My poor friends, I thought. What a shitty way to spend a week in Cambridge . . . I tried to imagine what you guys were up to when I was in Evin . . .'

Four months after Dorothy was released, the quartet of Hanger Sisters reassembled from three continents to meet up in Cambridge again for a long weekend, to finally have the reunion we had meant to have in May. Andrea, Julie and I were both elated and daunted at the prospect of the reunion. I mean, what do you say to a friend who, since you have last seen her, has been incarcerated by two governments in two countries and who has had experiences you want to know about but are afraid to ask, lest they cause unintentional trauma?

'Special dispensation,' D said, when we finally met, holding out her arms. 'Hugging with touching.'

That weekend, we did all the things we always do when we get together. Gossip. Get the low-down on our various romances and partners. Swap news about other classmates. Talk about work. Talk about writing projects. Drink cocktails. Drink more cocktails. Tell stories. Hit the designer resale boutiques. Complain about the person who gets tired of trawling through the consignment shops first. Bicker about where we'll eat that evening. Go looking for happy-hour oysters. Make sure we go at least once for *pho ga*. Talk about future plans. Bemoan the fact we have so little time together. Tell each other (or at least Andrea and I do an excellent ham double-act on this) that we will be repeatedly sticking virtual daggers in our hearts at the grief of separation upon departure.

Finally, in some dim bar in downtown Boston that week-end, the three of us looked at D as one over our Martinis.

'Tell us.'

'Tell us what it was like.'

'Are you really OK?'

We sat back and waited.

'When I had done the Al Jazeera interview, I came back to the apartment and finally looked at my email,' Dorothy said. She told us how overcome she had been when hundreds and hundreds of emails started loading, with their links to the many articles written about her and to the televised appeals by her family. That was before she had even been aware of the existence of the campaign to free her, as none of those emails, of course, was ever sent to her.

'I got down on the floor,' she said. 'I was totally over-whelmed. There had been days when I wondered if anyone had been missing me at all.' She had been absolutely undone by her inbox and the evidence of the worldwide efforts made to release her. 'You have to remember, this was the first time I had seen my email since I had left Doha to fly to Damascus. I had had no idea what had been going on.'

Her story came out in bits and pieces. As an Iranian passport-holder, she had not needed a visa to enter Syria and that passport had been duly stamped at immigration. But a scan of her luggage had revealed she had both a satellite phone and an internet hub with her, something which prompted the nervy authorities at the airport to thoroughly search her belongings. She had entered with her Iranian passport, but the subsequent search also turned up her American passport, which had her Al Jazeera-sponsored visa in it.

'They couldn't decide which was worse, that I was possibly an American spy for Israel or that I was an Al Jazeera reporter.'

D had not been held for any period of time at a nice, bland, clean anonymous conference room in Damascus airport. She had been shoved into a vehicle and taken, not to her hotel, as they told her they were doing, but to one of Syria's notorious secret prisons. On arrival there, they pulled her out of the vehicle by her hair, the first indication of what was to come.

She was blindfolded, handcuffed, taken to a courtyard, stood against a wall and left there to listen helplessly to the sounds of men being interrogated and beaten savagely. Dorothy knew some Arabic, enough to know what the men were crying out was, 'No!' and 'I swear to God!' It occurred to her that she might be next, either to be beaten or to be shot.

'My brain was in meltdown,' she said frankly. All the possibilities of the things that could happen to her next went through her head. That she might be shot dead. That she might be subjected to a mock execution. That she, too, might be beaten. In between these horrific thoughts, the sound of the men close to her being beaten drilled through her consciousness. There was something sticky under her feet. Through a crack in her blindfold, she saw it was blood.

Her first interrogation came at midnight on the first night, for four hours. Who was she, what was she doing in Syria, who did she really work for; who was she spying for, what were their names?

'What did you tell him?' we asked.

'The truth,' she said. 'That I was a journalist, not a spy. I only ever told the truth.'

After three days, she was told she was free to return to Qatar. That, of course, is not what happened.

'Bait and switch,' D said. 'They got me to the airport and then I realized at the gate that the plane was going to Tehran, not Doha.'

She tried to escape, but there were two armed guards and a minder who had been sent to accompany her on the flight. There was no escape to be had. It had never occurred to me that a passenger on an international scheduled flight – it was Caspian Airlines, the Iranian national airline – could be forced to board a plane against their will. But it turns out, when you are accompanied by armed guards, even if you are screaming and kicking and struggling, nobody is going to question those guards.

In Iran, she was brought straight to Evin and placed in solitary confinement. By the time I was reading the first emails in Dublin about Dorothy's disappearance, she was already in prison in Iran and had already undergone the first of many, many, round-the-clock interrogations. She was taken out of her cell blindfolded every time. She never saw the face of her interrogator.

'They changed the time every day. Sometimes it was midnight, sometimes six a.m., sometimes afternoon. I never knew when they were coming for me.'

On the morning of her first full day at Evin, she was brought before a judge, who reminded her that a charge of spying carried the death penalty in Iran. Dorothy did not need to be reminded of this. Unknown to me, she had had an obituary of Zahra Kazemi pinned over her desk for years, the Iranian-Canadian photojournalist who had died in Evin whom I had read about that terrible day back in May.

'He tried to get me to confess to being a spy. Then he told me, "We don't need to get a confession to execute you."'

Day after day, Dorothy kept insisting she was a journalist, not a spy. They went through many, many articles she had written, looking for criticism of the Iranian government. They made her give them all her email passwords and spent days reading her mail.

'I kept asking them if there was any news about me being missing, or any emails from my family, and they were vague and said, "Some." Then one day, my interrogator said to me, "You have a Wikipedia page." I was like: I have a Wikipedia page? Because I knew I hadn't before I arrived in Syria. That's the only time I thought that maybe something was happening in the outside world that I wasn't aware of.'

Along with the constant grillings about her alleged spying activities, Dorothy's interrogator threw some bizarre questions into the mix.

'What was my favourite colour? What had that to do with anything? Turns out, he had gone through my suitcase. He wanted to know why all my clothes were black. He said I must be very modest. I told him it was my favourite colour, and he told me black was not a colour and why didn't I wear any colours? He couldn't figure that out.'

In the downtown Boston bar that we were in, the four of us laughed our heads off. Dorothy was, of course, wearing black as she told us this.

'Why was I a vegetarian?

'Why did I wear so much black?

'Why had I chosen to have a career instead of getting married and staying at home?'

In the end, it seems they decided she was not a spy. They

read the many articles we wrote about Dorothy and watched the broadcasts and listened to audio; the consistent message was she was simply a journalist with multiple citizenships. But who knows how such people make these decisions? I wouldn't dare guess, especially since other Westerners have remained and still remain incarcerated in Evin for far longer. Dorothy was eventually put on a dawn flight to Doha from Tehran nineteen days after going missing.

'They gave me a farewell gift. Three boxes of Gaz, Iranian nougat I used to love as a kid. I mean, the people who locked me up and told me they could kill me gave me candy when they let me go?' Dorothy shook her head, still confounded by the contradiction, by the final surreality of the most intense days of her life.

It's a decade now since all that happened. Dorothy eventually left Qatar. She works as an editor for NPR (National Public Radio) now, in Washington DC. I'm the only one of us four still working for the same paper I was back when we were Niemans.

Julie left the *Monterey County Herald* when the lay-offs and cutbacks annihilated the paper to the extent that it was no longer a functioning entity, not to mention that it had abandoned its reporting ethics. Andrea hung on quite a bit longer, but she left the *Plain Dealer* when the same miserable thing happened there. They both still work as reporters on freelance projects, but they both miss like hell the adrenaline and buzz of working on newspapers. I have survivor guilt sometimes when we meet up, although, of course, the ultimate survivor among us is Dorothy.

We Hanger Sisters are closer than ever. I guess the four of us are bonded for life now or, as Dorothy said the last time I met up with her and Andrea, 'You're my ride-or-die friends.' I had to ask her what the expression meant. It's pretty cool, actually. And it's true. You don't go through something like that together and then fall out or lose touch or forget about each other.

Something momentous happened that ride-or-die last time three of the four of us met up. Andrea and I were visiting D, who had taken the weekend off work to be with us. But of course, we wanted to see her workplace, so we dragged her back into the NPR office on North Capitol Street, the office she was meant to be having a break from.

We toured the former telecommunications building with our nerdy journalist hats on: there is nothing more fascinating for reporters than seeing what other newsrooms look like. It was, flat out, the most creative-looking space I've ever seen, with a piano in one workspace and whiteboards of ideas and an old-fashioned booth in the open-plan area to take private calls in, and Post-its and a pen in the Ladies to write things to stick on the mirror, like the poshest version of graffiti ever.

It was a Saturday, and D's show, the *Weekend Edition*, hosted that day by Scott Simon, was on air as we nosed around the office.

'Would you like to sit in for a while?' she asked us.

Andrea and I were through that studio door like horses out of the traps during Cheltenham. The three of us sat quietly together at the back, watching the editors and producers working and Scott Simon in the adjacent glass-fronted studio with some interviewees around a table. Like all magazine shows, it was a mix of pre-recorded pieces and live interviews, a highly choreographed process, down to the second.

But suddenly, there was a kerfuffle, with a lot of back-and-forth speaking through headphones. D's head snapped up like a meerkat's. She knew something unusual was happening. We exchanged glances. There was breaking news and a planned section of the show was being dropped so that they could patch in their White House reporter, who was awaiting a press conference there.

And so it was we were sitting in that studio together when the then President, Donald Trump, announced the first death from Covid-19 in the US. It was 29 February 2020. We had no idea then what was before us all, nor how this was to be the first of many, many deaths to occur in the US and around the world. How air travel would change so drastically and how it would seem bizarre to consider visiting someone else's workplace when so many of us now, including me, work from home and haven't seen their own office in months. The day I'm writing this, the US has just recorded a quarter of a million deaths from Covid-19, and it's clear the pandemic is far from over.

I don't know when I'll see my Hanger Sisters again. But I do know there will never be enough time to talk about all the things we want to talk about. Our friendship is one of the biggest joys of my life. I know that these three people will be in my life for ever.

What I don't know, and never will, is what being disappeared for nineteen days does to a person afterwards, along with the underlying and constant fear that you could be executed or tortured or imprisoned for years. Only Dorothy knows that.

BOOK FRIENDS

BOOKS HAVE ALWAYS been my friends, and always will be. Reading remains a singular joy in my life, as it surely must be for everyone else who also loves books. You are alone but not alone, absorbed in the story and the world that someone else has created. I love my tech gadgets but have never downloaded any book other than guidebooks on my iPad when travelling. I also love podcasts and have an extensive library of them on my phone but, for some reason, I have never wanted to experiment with audiobooks.

No, it's actual, real books, with their heft and physicality, that I love. Some of them have been with me most of my life. In the hallway, there's a bookcase with the books I read and loved in childhood. In my kitchen-dining room, there are floor-to-ceiling bookcases. Some of the books in there I'll always keep, and they've been hauled around with me in boxes so many times from shared houses to rented flats and, eventually, to my own place. Others get given away, passed on, taken to charity shops. Those ones are my book friends in passing, not my book friends for life.

For everyone who loves books, some speak to us as if written just for us. Those books arrive in our lives at a time when they answer some important question or teach us something or give a very necessary kind of delight. Those books somehow lodge deep into our consciousness as time passes. Reading them at the time we read them becomes a life experience in itself; experiences that become more apparent as our lives continue.

Or so I have found it to be. There are some books whose spines I catch sight of and a stab of memory goes through me. I can't go back to the person I was when I first read them but the memory of that experience of first reading them remains and, most importantly, the feelings they provoked in me. They are my Proustian madeleines to the past, and these are just five of many.

Curiosity: The Guinness Book of Records *(1967)*

There was a big, heavy mahogany bookcase on the upstairs landing of the house I grew up in. It contained historical periodicals belonging to my father, a few hardback novels that had belonged to my long-dead grandmother – *The Key Above the Door, The Small Dark Man, Three Daughters of the United Kingdom* – and an overflow of books from elsewhere in the house.

On the bottom shelf, which was the tallest, there was a hardback 1967 *Guinness Book of Records*. I don't know where it came from. Possibly one of my older brothers. It was without its dust jacket, although I didn't realize that then. The turquoise blue cover was very faded. The title on the spine was upside down: it read from bottom to top, instead of the usual way: downwards.

Some afternoon in childhood, I took it out from the packed shelf one afternoon when I had temporarily run out of books to read. There were some pictures, I noted on first opening it, but nothing like enough. Then I began to flick through it.

Within five minutes, I was absolutely absorbed. The amount of detail was staggering. There were so many facts inside this book. So many peculiar stories. So many people who had done such strange things.

From time to time, I would return to this book and flick through more pages. I couldn't read too much of it in one go. It was too much to take in, too dense. The entries were short but so many had the potential for entire novels. The man who had swallowed so many items. The woman who had so many children. The man who had such long fingernails. It was a book of treasures, a book for the curious. I had had no idea the world was so fascinating: that real people actually did these extraordinary things, or was it that extraordinary things happened to people?

Either way, I could not get enough of the *Guinness Book of Records* 1967. I pored over it for hours and hours. I learned such weird information about the world. I was reading it in the 1970s, so the records were all from some years previously, but they provided pointers to so many superlative actions I had never thought about before but now loved to know: the dog who had killed the most rats; where the biggest toyshop in the world was; the most travelled man in the world; how much the most expensive perfume cost; the longest song title.

How did the *Guinness Book of Records* find out about all this stuff? I would wonder with fascination. If I tried to skip as long as I could, or eat some food item in large quantities, or ride my bike round and round the garden to clock up many miles, how would anyone know, other than me? How did they know when people performed record-breaking feats, and how did they find out how many people could fit into a railway waiting room in China, or where the brightest lighthouse in the world was, or who owned the most talkative budgie and how many words it said?

I felt the same awe and sense of endless possibility as I had the day it struck me that life had gone on before my existence and would continue after my death. Time did not end. Possibilities were endless. The world was full of detail, tiny, minute detail, so much so that someone had bothered to find out the most words a budgie could say and then put it in a book. Sometimes, I would put down the *Guinness Book of Records* and feel simultaneously exhausted and thrilled. Every single time I went back to it, I discovered another something new that made me marvel all over again. I kept feeding my curiosity by returning to the book.

Alas, that particular copy of the 1967 *Guinness Book of Records* vanished somewhere along the way. I made the mistake of not claiming it for myself. It got thrown out, most probably at the same time as did my mother's gorgeous *Vogue* and *Simplicity* pattern books, whose loss I still mourn.

So I went online a month ago and bought a copy on eBay for a few euros. The day it arrived – complete with fancy dust jacket – I could not stop reading it. If anything, it was an even more absorbingly randomly detailed portrait of a world that had existed over half a century ago.

I searched for the entry I remembered best, the one that had fascinated me the most: the man who had swallowed so many strange items. I used to imagine what all these items would look like laid out on the floor and how they could possibly fit into his stomach along with his dinner. Why had he done it?

The worst known case of compulsive swallowing was reported in the Journal of the American Medical Association *in December*

1960. The patient, who complained only of swollen ankles, was found to have 258 items in his stomach, including a 3-lb piece of metal, 26 keys, three sets of rosary beads, 16 religious medals, a bracelet, a necklace, three pairs of tweezers, four nail clippers, 39 nail files, three metal chains and 88 assorted coins.

I look at that entry now and realize at once: that man was not at all well in the head. Was he trying to perform some kind of religious mortification of the body, swallowing all those rosary beads and holy medals? But what about the nail files and clippers and tweezers, which hinted more at having belonged to a woman than a man? And the single bracelet and necklace? Who had owned that bracelet and necklace and why did he swallow those items? For revenge? To make some point? Did he return them to their owner once they came back out of his stomach? Would you want to wear a necklace and bracelet again, when you knew they had been in someone's stomach?

It is an entry that is even more disturbingly mystifying to me as an adult than when I first read it as a child and one that still provokes my curiosity.

By 1967, the *Guinness Book of Records* had been going for eleven years. The short preface thanked 'correspondents from some 150 countries for raising or settling various editorial points'. I notice now things that totally passed me by as a child. Words we don't use any more. Like 'Negress' and 'authoress' and 'murderess'. There are many extremely uncomfortable entries on body weight and women's waist size and slimming and suicide. The very first entry in the book is for 'Tallest Giants', and 'giantesses' are also listed, as are 'shortest dwarfs'. There is an entry for a 'face-slapping contest' in Kiev which lasted thirty hours and another for the longest distance achieved by a 'human cannon ball', which was 155 feet by a member of the Ringling Brothers and Barnum & Bailey Circus.

I read on gingerly, wincing now and then at the crassness of some of the entries: the 'smallest brain', for instance, was to be found in an 'microcephalous idiot'.

And yet there still remained so many odd jewels, as well as quite startling pieces of information. The last person in France to be guillotined – and not only guillotined, but publicly so – was at Versailles before a large crowd of people on 17 June 1939, less than thirty years before the publication of the book I was now reading. I was absolutely astounded. I had believed the guillotine went out with the French Revolution. I had to immediately google Eugen Weidmann to see what crimes he had committed. He was a German-born man who worked with two other men to kidnap, rob and murder rich tourists in France. Maybe everyone else knows that gruesome piece of information, but I certainly did not.

I texted my friend Tanya after I read that detail, asking if she knew when the last person in France had been guillotined. She's used to me texting her random non-sequiturs. We did a deep dive of the internet after that. It turns out that Eugen Weidmann was not in fact the last person to be guillotined in France. That horrible distinction went to a man called Hamida Djandoubi, who was executed in that way a full decade after the 1967 *Guinness Book of Records* was published, on 10 September 1977.

The man with the longest fingernails, whom I remembered from childhood, was a Chinese priest. His nails were almost twenty-three inches long, a horrible feat that had taken him twenty-seven years to achieve. The dog who had killed all those shudderingly many rats – the whole one thousand in under two hours – was called Jacko. I remembered his name because I had so wanted a dog myself as a child, but not one that had anything to do with rats.

I read with amazement and envy that the highest rate ever offered to a writer for one article by that point was to Ernest Hemingway in 1960. It was for *Sports Illustrated*, a publication still in operation, and he got paid $30,000, the equivalent of $15 a word. The piece was on bullfighting. Even today, that is a staggering sum. Back in 1960, it would have been astonishing riches. I hope they got their money's worth: I've never read it.

Communism was, of course, still in existence. Back then, the largest stadium in the world was recorded as being in Prague: the Strahov Stadium. It could accommodate an incredible 240,000 spectators for 'mass displays of up to 40,000 Sokol gymnasts'. I had to google 'Sokol' to find out what the word meant: a 'Slav gymnastic society aiming to promote a communal spirit and physical fitness, originating in Prague in 1862'. The stadium is still there and was put on UNESCO's cultural heritage sites list in 2003. It's used for concerts now.

I lost a whole day dipping in and out of the book I had loved so much in childhood. Or did I lose it? No, I spent a whole day reminding myself of the kind of trivia and random facts and tiny, unfinished stories I still love so much to absorb. It was not a lost day.

Words came unbidden into my head from one of my favourite Louis MacNeice poems, 'Snow':

> *World is crazier and more of it than we think,*
> *Incorrigibly plural.*

Adventure: The Slow Train to Milan, by Lisa St Aubin de Terán (1983)

Whenever I buy a book, I almost always write my name and the date and place I bought it on the flyleaf. I see now I bought my paperback Penguin copy of *The Slow Train to Milan* in London, September 1989, for £3.99. I was twenty-four back then.

The Slow Train to Milan is classified as fiction, but I never believed it was anything other than embroidered memoir. Everything from the narrator's name being Lisaveta, when the author's name was Lisa, to the biographical note at the beginning:

> At the age of sixteen, she left James Allen's Girls' School to marry. She and her exiled Venezuelan husband travelled for two years in Italy before returning to his family home in the Andes. During her seven years in South America, she managed her husband's sugar plantation and avocado farm . . .

On the very first page, Lisaveta, aged sixteen and still at school, meets an exiled Venezuelan man on a street close to her home. She has been running errands and is carrying a wicker basket.

The man – Cesar, nineteen years older – steps in front of her and announces by way of introduction, 'South America.' Then he takes her shopping basket, walks her back to the flat, where she is alone in the absence of her mother, and simply moves in. He speaks hardly any English. Three days later, he asks her to marry him. Two more exiled Venezuelan friends of

Cesar's show up, Otto and Elias. They are all, he tells Lisaveta, 'bank robbers' on the run.

Within months, Cesar and Lisaveta are married and, with Otto and Elias, begin a peripatetic two years of shuttling across Europe on the slow train to Milan, mostly backwards and forwards between Paris and Bologna. Nothing much happens in this book and everything that does happens over and over again like in a Beckett play.

And yet I loved this book so much I read it probably ten times in my mid-twenties. When I was sixteen, I was at a convent boarding school in the Irish Midlands and knew nothing about anything. I'm not sure I knew much more at twenty-four, when I bought this book. Lisaveta already had eight years of living on me by then.

I read it as an adventure story, a memoir that ended on the brink of another adventure when the protagonist was barely twenty and sailing across the Atlantic to South America. Our names were not dissimilar; Rosita/Lisaveta. Lisaveta left everything of her former life behind to become one of this gang of four: her planned Oxbridge education, her family, albeit scattered hither and thither.

I envied Lisaveta's ability to abandon both her past and her planned future with such dedication. I had from time to time considered dropping out of my college education, which I was not enjoying, but had lacked the courage to do so. I also envied her significant self-containment and seeming lack of a need for friends, other than the two plus her husband she was wandering around Europe with. She does not namecheck a single female friend in the entire book. In fact, she mentions her friends only when they prove impossible to find, as when she and Cesar turn up in Paris to discover that the hotel she used to stay in had been demolished.

In fact, she tells us, in a casual aside, she used to live in Paris. How did she once live in Paris and yet also attend school in London? But I rushed past this confusing conflicting information to the incantation of her exotic Parisian friends whom she and Cesar took taxis across the city to try and find: the pop singer, the nuclear physicist, the professor, the actor and the journalist from the Associated Press, who 'always ate on the corner where the Mafia ate'. Such an assortment of friends! Even though, it turned out, none was in, or contactable afterwards. Did they even exist? I began to wonder.

Lisaveta did not travel light. No modern rucksack for her, like the one I had. She travelled with heavy leather suitcases, including more than one just for her books, notebooks and writing materials. This, too, in a fantasy world, was exactly how I wanted to travel. A couple of years after I first read *The Slow Train to Milan*, I went to Scotland for Hogmanay to visit my friend Alexander. I took with me, in homage to Lisa/ Lisaveta, my father's brown leather suitcase, which he had had in boarding school, a case which had his initials on it.

It was heavy even with nothing in it and I had trouble lifting it by myself when it was full. Alexander and I hauled this ridiculous weight on to trains from Edinburgh to Inverness, and across the Drumochter Pass to Ullapool, drinking from a hip flask of whisky and telling stories as the snowy mountains rose out of the wintry gloaming around us. It was the only journey I ever took that suitcase on.

In the book, money is always tight; they live on Lisaveta's allowance from her academic, long-divorced father, until it runs out. They behave appallingly in the rented accommodation they lurch from: their bills include breakages and damage to property, as if they were spectacularly poorly behaved rock stars of a certain era. They shoplift as a matter of course, and Cesar pawns Lisaveta's jewellery without her knowledge – her five antique rings, in amber, garnet, moonstone, cameo and jade – but holds on to his own. I would have been raging; she accepts their loss. None of the characters are very likable, even Lisaveta, and I never fully understood why the three men were on the run.

Still, I kept going back to the book. Pleasingly, Lisaveta mostly wore vintage Edwardian long, floating clothes, dresses made of velvet and silk, along with boots and hats and fur wraps. I, too, loved vintage clothes. I had a slub 1940s silk ivory wedding dress with a long train I had bought for a tenner in a London charity shop and worn not at all ironically to several parties, the train hooked up either side of my waist to resemble shepherdess panniers. I had soft brown high Italian boots that laced up in the Victorian manner, and I wore them all the time. I had large velvet hats. I had elbow-length gloves in black velvet, and ones in silver lamé with a row of pearl buttons, and another in cerise-pink satin, and ivory kid gloves that rolled up on to my fingers like butter.

I had tulle underskirts that made the skirts of my dresses look like crinolines. I wore to a wedding, completely without self-consciousness, a dyed silk-satin bias-cut sleeveless night-dress that had belonged to Nancy's grandmother. I had many shawls. What I really, really wanted was a long black satin or woollen cloak, lined with scarlet or orange silk, but I never found one. There was nothing I longed for more than to sit on European trains with my leather suitcase full of books, wearing my vintage charity-shop finds and my mother's dress gloves from the 1960s, and have adventures with men from another continent, one of them my extremely exotic husband.

The Slow Train to Milan is suffused with the oddest of extravagances and the most profound solipsism on the part of all four characters. For a time, it is English-speaking Lisaveta's task to go to a phone box and call a bank in London to see if a cable for the incredible sum of $340,000 had arrived for Cesar. It never arrived. She tells us that the best gift she ever bought Cesar was a box of five hundred mother-of-pearl buttons, as he refused to wear shirts without these exact kind of buttons. At one point, she lies on a mattress for days, terribly ill and bleeding with some unspecified 'kidney' problem – or, more likely, as I suspected, a miscarriage – and she is more or less left there by herself. I couldn't work out if she was simply passive and let everything happen to her or if she somehow created these scenarios by choice.

And throughout it all, they kept aimlessly riding the slow train to Milan. Lisaveta states that there were only two certainties in her life: long dresses and moving on. 'The extravagance of the clothes and the comfort of the travel.' I envied her those separate, random certainties at a time in my life when I wasn't sure what my certainties were, other than that I wanted adventures. I wanted to wear vintage clothes full time and marry a stranger who accosted me on the street, and ride trains, and burn documents and forged passports, and run from the law and hang out with a gang of men from a country I knew nothing about, and then go to live on a sugar plantation in Venezuela, which I would manage myself.

Most of all, I loved that the central character of this improbable travel book was a young woman. All the travel books I was reading back then were by men; Jonathan Raban, Bruce

Chatwin, Paul Theroux, Bill Bryson. I enjoyed them all a lot for different reasons, but none of those male narrators spoke to me like Lisaveta did in *The Slow Train to Milan*. She was undeniably unbelievably exotic, but at least half her exoticism for me was that she was a young woman traveller and writer.

I had read and admired Dervla Murphy, but knew that Dervla Murphy, with her fierce independence and her hiking and cycling and mule-riding, would never, ever have wanted to wear a long velvet dress on her travels. She would never have shuttled backwards and forwards on trains to no end. She would never be waiting for a cable of money that never came. She would have made mincemeat of the four of them. I didn't want to have her austere adventures. I wanted folly and companionship and trains and velvet dresses.

Above all, what I loved about the *The Slow Train to Milan* was its pointlessness and its absurdity, but also how it was watermarked throughout with a non-judgemental ethos. Yes, Lisaveta made mistakes. But the mistakes and the lack of focus were an integral part of her messy story. There were no bragging rights here, as there were, both in the subtext and in the text itself, in the journeys of the men whose travel books I read: of taking a boat down the Mississippi; or travelling grumpily across a continent by train, ticking off countries as he went; or going to Patagonia with self-aggrandizement to hunt for the brontosaurus that turned out to be a sloth.

The Slow Train to Milan was not about bravado, or a journey embarked upon with an advance set purpose, or a preposterous quest story. It was the story of an unplanned, chaotic and spontaneous adventure, the kind of adventure I longed to have myself: such adventures I have since had; adventures I am still constantly seeking.

Incompletion: Island, *by Alistair MacLeod (2000)*

In 2001, I went to a fancy dinner in Dublin Castle. It was an awards dinner for what was then called the International IMPAC Dublin Literary Award. Nobody was ever quite sure who IMPAC were, except they very generously sponsored the world's most valuable prize for a single work of fiction. This monetary award was for £100,000.

I had been to this dinner in previous years. It was lavish and formal and involved harpists playing in the Portrait Gallery as guests arrived, said guests, including me, trying not to look too eager (definitely me) as we accepted the proffered glasses of champagne. It was an excellent excuse to dress up and meet colleagues from the media and publishing world and celebrate literature.

The writer who had won that year was the Canadian author Alistair MacLeod, who had grown up on Cape Breton, for his novel *No Great Mischief*. We already knew who had won: that announcement had been made some weeks previously. His name was unfamiliar to me back then. That was unsurprising, as he had published only three books in total: two collections of short stories and this now-celebrated novel. His name was not well known on the European side of the Atlantic at that time, or it certainly wasn't by me. *No Great Mischief* had taken him thirteen years to write. He was then sixty-five.

When the bell had been rung and we had belatedly faux politely craned our necks to look at the table plans pinned up on a board, we all finally found our seats. To my delight, there was a signed copy of *No Great Mischief* on every place setting. I carefully put mine away in my bag and relaxed into the evening. It was in the days before the smoking ban and there were ashtrays on the tables. Clouds of smoke soon began to waft up to the ceiling of St Patrick's Hall.

Alistair MacLeod was ruddy and smiley and looked as Scottish as his name suggested, although he was born in Canada many generations after his ancestors had left Scotland. He had a tumbler of whiskey in his hand. I recall him wearing a tweed cap with his tuxedo, but perhaps that is because every publicity photograph of him shows him wearing a cap. His grown-up children, who had come over with him to support their father's life work, had the reddest of red auburn hair.

In former years, once the presentation had been made and the speeches given and the coffees served, people drifted away into the insubstantial night. But that year was different. That year, Alistair MacLeod, his wife and their family of red-haired children left their tables, went out into the adjacent Portrait Gallery and began to play music. The dinner guests, including me, who would usually be heading downstairs to the cloakroom by then, to retrieve coats and make a departure, did not leave.

We abandoned our tables as one and went as if magnetized to the Portrait Gallery, where we found the source of that wild, furious, elegiac music. The grown-up red-haired children of Alistair MacLeod were playing fiddles and singing; tunes and songs that sounded subliminally Irish but weren't. It was the music of Scotland and the music of Cape Breton, the songs and tunes that went out across the ocean with the families who emigrated from Scotland at around the same time the building we were in had been constructed, in the 1770s; the families belonging to Alistair MacLeod who settled on the remote and sea-washed islands of Cape Breton and Nova Scotia and who became a displaced clan, the clan which I was later to discover Alistair MacLeod wrote all his fiction about.

We stood in the Portrait Gallery and the sound of that music crashed over our heads like waves. It was haunting and dangerous and magnificent all at once.

Alistair MacLeod stood solid that evening among his family, watching and smiling and listening, a steadfast rock of a man in a moiling ocean of history.

When I read the book not long after that dinner, I found myself crying near the end; the only other novel I have wept over as much is William Trevor's masterful *The Story of Lucy Gault*. *No Great Mischief* is a superb, lyrical fable of a family who emigrated from Scotland in the eighteenth century and the clan they begot. It's about survival in its many fraught manifestations and about the ceaselessly painful ways one can suffer in a family when one seeks familial love, a complicated love that is frequently, although not always, unforthcoming.

Scenes from the novel did indeed sear into my memory; uppermost among them is the particularly beautiful and terrible set piece where three members of the same family vanish under formerly solid ice one winter night on their way home. The final line of *No Great Mischief* is: 'All of us are better when we're loved.'

I talked avidly about this book to many of my friends, encouraging them to read it. One friend then asked to borrow my copy. I broke my own rules about never lending books and gave it to her. The book that eventually came back to me two years later was not the book I had loaned out.

'It was signed. My copy was signed.' I was stupidly distraught.

'No, it's the same one,' this friend insisted. 'I never even got round to reading it.'

'My copy was signed,' I repeated stoutly, staring at the unsigned title page of a book I had not seen for more than two years, nor looked at the inside pages of for upwards of another further year. Then I began to doubt that the copy left on my place mat on the night of the awards dinner had actually been signed. Except, I had been so certain it was. Had I imagined it? Why would my friend lie? Had I imagined something I thought was true but in fact was not?

Sometime later, I bought *Island*. Alistair MacLeod wrote two collections of stories, each with just seven stories. *The Lost Salt Gift of Blood* was published in 1976 and *As Birds Bring Forth the Sun* in 1986. *Island* gathered these two collections in one book, along with two additional stories he had written later, in 1988 and 1999. That, and *No Great Mischief*, is his entire output.

The stories are all set in Cape Breton and each one has the range of a novel. They are defined by the ocean and the things that are unsaid in families, and by manual labour and people being married to each other who should never have married each other. They are so beautiful and so painful to read.

When I got to the fifth story in the collection of sixteen, 'The Fall', I stopped four pages in. The story opens with the portentous sentence: ' "We'll just have to sell him," I remember my mother saying with finality.'

The 'him' is their horse, Scott. Within those four pages, it is evident that this is another marriage that should never have happened, that the child narrator has grown up with the horse and that his father, a miner, has rescued this horse from the mine and loves him. The mother considers the horse now worthless and an expensive large extra mouth to feed in a hard winter. The horse is a symbol for all that is not right in this family.

I don't know how the rest of the story pans out, because I never finished it. I didn't read any more of the book. I couldn't. It was a day when I was feeling vulnerable and I didn't want to make myself feel even sadder. So I put *Island* on the shelf beside my unsigned *No Great Mischief*, and there it has remained ever since.

From time to time, like now, I take it down and contemplate finishing it. The book always opens at the place where I stopped reading, on page 101. I just can't do it. It's not the only book I have never finished, but it is the only book I did not finish because I knew I could not bear to read any more. It was too superb and too hard to read because the pain and truth and longing in the stories spoke so keenly to me.

Over the years since, *Island* has become, in its own way, a symbol for all the other uncompleted things in my life that are too painful to think about often. The children I never had. The friends I lost. The relationships I could not see to the end. The promises I did not keep. The opportunities I let go. The time I wasted.

I can never let that book go; it will always stay on my shelves. Maybe someday, when I am old and grey and full of sleep and nodding by the fire, I will take down *Island* and finish it. And maybe then I will learn something I should really know about now, something that I don't need to be scared of, something that will be redemptive. But not now. Not just yet.

Alistair MacLeod will never sign any more books. He died in 2014, aged seventy-seven. *No Great Mischief* remains his only novel. At his funeral, the final line on the memorial service programme read: 'All of us are better when we're loved.'

Perspectives: Lighthouse, *by Tony Parker (1975)*

Along with my name, I've written 'Dublin, February 1987' on the flyleaf of my copy of *Lighthouse*. I was in my final year in college then. The book cost £4.95.

Tony Parker was an oral historian, an absolutely superlative one. I did not understand what an oral historian was back then. The biographical note read: 'He has written many books of a documentary nature, all of them based like this on tape-recorded interviews – a technique he has pioneered and made his own, and which was described by the *Times Literary Supplement* in a review of contemporary literature as "the one genuine new art form of the past decade".'

Lighthouse, which Parker researched and wrote in the early 1970s, is a series of interviews with lighthouse keepers across Britain and, sometimes, also their wives. (Lighthouse-keeping was an exclusively male job.) He documented the last generation of men to do this job. Within two decades, they would all be replaced by computers and automation.

Being a lighthouse keeper sounds like the most romantic of occupations, which is precisely why I bought this book. Like many people, I initially thought there was something noble and mysterious and man-against-nature about being a lighthouse keeper; living in the middle of extreme weather, surrounded by ocean. But Parker makes it clear right from his introduction that not only is the job mostly mind-blowingly boring, repetitive and lonely, it also has its own rigid and soul-destroying inescapable hierarchy twenty-four hours a day.

It took Parker three years to get permission from Trinity House to visit island and tower lights; land lights, being not dependent on sea travel, were more accessible. Trinity House, which was – and still is – based in London, is the organization once wholly responsible for overseeing lighthouse operations around Britain and Ireland. It built its first lighthouse in 1609, at Lowestoft in Suffolk.

Parker's research trips to various 'lights' – as lighthouses were known – across Britain took six months. We never know the names of the buildings he visits. He says in his acknowledgements that the descriptions of life at the three different kinds of lights are 'composite pictures, and not descriptions of specific stations'.

At its core, *Lighthouse* comprises a series of interviews with men at different stages of their careers at each of the three different types of lights. Parker also interviews the wives of some of these men, and other people who work for Trinity House, such as the boatmen who bring the keepers out and those whose jobs are to periodically visit to maintain the lights. We never know the real names of any of the many people he interviews, any more than the names of the lighthouses he visited. His method of working was devised to guarantee his interviewees anonymity.

In 1578, the Skellig Michael rock passed to the Butler family in County Kerry not long after the Dissolution of the Monasteries. Back in 1820, when Ireland was under British rule, Trinity House approved Skellig Michael, off the Kerry coast, as a location for two rock lighthouses, an upper and a lower. The following year, it was estimated that the rock was worth £780, the equivalent of £86,000 today. The Butler family decided to sell Skellig Michael to Trinity House.

The two lights were duly built, each of them with cottages

attached. The lower light, which could be seen from a distance of eighteen miles, had two attached houses, one for the Principal Keeper and the other for the Assistant Keeper. On 4 December 1826, the lights went on for the first time at Skelligs. In 1870, the upper light was taken out of commission.

They were still being manned when I went there for the first time, as a child of six or seven, in the early 1970s, around the same time Tony Parker was conducting his research for *Lighthouse*. We went for several summer holidays to Bunavalla, an impossibly scenic place close to Derrynane in County Kerry. We saw the pyramid-shaped islands on the horizon on Sundays when we drove into Waterville after attending Mass at Loher church.

The seafaring O'Shea family of Bunavalla had – and still retain – the skippering rights to take people out to the Skelligs from Derrynane pier. One calm summer day, my father and I embarked for the two-hour boat journey out with John O'Shea and some six or so other passengers. The routine was two hours out, two hours on the island and two hours back. There were, of course, no life jackets or life raft back then on *L'Oursin*, a boat I knew, because my brothers had told me, was a 'half decker'. It was my first time on a boat journey of any distance. I remember being very excited and very cold. Despite the warm day, the wind went right through my T-shirt, cardigan and shorts.

Although I did not realize it at the time, along with her passengers, *L'Oursin* was carrying some supplies for the lighthouse keepers who were still attending the light on Skellig Michael back then. The tourist boats went only in summer and, even then, only on those unpredictable days when the

Atlantic was calm enough for the six-hour round trip, as it was on the day I went out as a child.

My impressions of the Skelligs were of a wholly vertical place, both from a distance and close up. When our boat arrived into tiny Blind Man's Cove, it took several minutes for us all to disembark, so choppy was the water and so wildly did the boat lurch up and down. John O' swung me ashore to waiting arms.

'If you're not back on time, I'll go without you!' John O' joked, once we were all safely on land, a stock line he used every time. I did not know then that this was a joke. The idea of being left behind in this vertical place it had taken two hours by boat to reach was terrifying.

We climbed the many stone steps to the stone beehive huts near the top of Skellig Michael. The sense of isolation from the world I knew was overwhelming. I was utterly confounded when my father told me that monks had lived in these stone huts long ago. It seemed the antithesis of home in every way. Why would anyone want to live there?

I do not remember seeing the lighthouse that day, or even being aware that it was there. I do remember frequently asking my father to check his watch so that we would get back to the boat on time and we would not get left behind.

There are so many elements of genius in the writing of *Lighthouse*, but one is Parker's decision to examine conflicting points of view, different perspectives. He talks to the keepers and also to the wives of those who were married. Each tell vastly different stories of the same job and the same marriage. In the same way the first male astronauts went to the moon and left their family lives behind, it was similarly impossible for those women the lighthouse keepers left behind to ever physically or emotionally travel to where their men spent so much of their working lives.

The top job was Principal Keeper (PK); a job that became open only on either the death or retirement of an incumbent; the in-between job was Assistant Keeper (AK); and the dogsbody role was the ultimate job title in civil-service gobbledegook, 'Supernumerary Assistant Keeper' (SAK). Even when you reached the role of Principal Keeper, your security vanished again, as this meant another series of years in tower lights, the most difficult posting of all. Each light, at any one time, had three men in these separate roles in residence, with two men subservient to one.

The lights themselves were split into three distinct types: land lights, rock lights and tower lights. Land lights were located on the mainland, frequently remote but still on land, which meant families could live together. These were by far the most coveted postings. Rock lights were on small islands that allowed one to walk around outside or go fishing or have a vegetable patch, but families could not go. Tower lights were man-made constructions atop a sea-washed rock and the only time you went in and out the door you were winched up through was when you were 'going off' – which actually meant coming on duty, as in going offshore – or leaving at the end of eight weeks, which was termed 'coming ashore'.

The more stories Parker tells, the more you realize how nobody understands what the necessarily immersive job of a lighthouse keeper is except other keepers, and then only some of them, depending on their individual personalities and temperament.

Margaret, aged fifty-two, was the wife of a Principal Keeper,

Stanley, who had been in the service for thirty years. At the time of her interview, he was stationed on a rock light, which was in sight of the cottage on the shore where they lived. In summer, every week she went out on a local tourist boat that makes a circuit of the rock so she could wave at him. This ritual was important to her and made her feel close to him, she told Parker.

But in Stanley's interview, which Parker conducted out on the rock light, where he spent some days, Stanley said that he dreaded when Margaret came out on one of these tourist boats to wave at him. 'I haven't the heart to tell her I wish she wouldn't because it upsets me for days.' For him, it's 'like purgatory'. On calm days after the boat had been out and they had waved to each other, Stanley revealed he was so lonely and distressed that he had to stop himself wanting to swim to shore after her. 'I'm not the sort of man who can live on his own, I need my wife.'

Stanley's interview is so very sad. It's the record of a man who has the self-knowledge to admit he made a 'bad mistake' in joining the service. He talked about thirty wasted years in the job and of being institutionalized and feeling trapped. He said that the only useful skill he learned in all that time was how to make ships in bottles, a craft he learned from the Principal Keeper he was once under. He said the only thing he was proud of was providing for their only child, a daughter who wanted to study medicine, but that shouldn't be anything to be proud of; he was doing no more than any parent should. He called his wife Margaret his 'only friend'.

Stanley also admitted he now bullied the younger men, the Supernumerary Assistant Keepers, in the same way he once was bullied by men who had his current position of

Principal Keeper, even though he despised himself for doing so. With blunt candour, Stanley told Parker he knew he gave the last SAK 'a dog's life', but that he simply couldn't help himself.

Stanley was clearly so irreparably burned out from the job that it is almost painful to read of his honesty and despair and his admirable desire throughout to try to be the best man he can for his wife and child.

The detail Parker manages to extrapolate is simultaneously so granular and so illustrative. It's a book without a single photograph, but every page is so richly visual. At one point he lists the food supplies for fifty-six days that Stanley habitually ordered to take out with him. It included 12 tins of sausages, 16 lbs of sugar, 24 Oxo cubes, 36 assorted tins of spaghetti, 24 eggs, 18 boxes of matches and a staggering 1,000 cigarettes. Every man Parker interviewed seemed to be a habitual heavy smoker, whether they rolled their own or smoked ready-mades, which must have meant that, on tower lights, there was a permanent and inescapable smell of cigarette smoke.

Less than a decade after I first visited Skellig Michael, on 22 April 1981, the lighthouse there became automated. In 1989, the Irish State bought Skellig Michael from the Commissioners of Irish Lights, but the commissioners retained both the lighthouse site itself and its surrounding area. Maintenance for the island passed to the Office of Public Works, which still has responsibility for the greater area of Skelligs, including the historic beehive huts, and which controls the number of visitors allowed to land there on any one day.

In 2005, I was working on a personal project that involved writing one story on all the thirty-two counties in Ireland.

When it came to Kerry, it was the Skelligs that kept coming back to me: I had been back to the rock once since, during the summer of 1987 after I had finished in college. I had spent that summer living with my brother David and working in Ted Butler's bar in Caherdaniel. It was Ted's great-grandfather who had sold Skellig Michael to Trinity House in the 1820s and, somehow, this was a fact I knew; it was part of local knowledge. Ted, a gruff, taciturn character with unruly hair, was still alive then, and he was often in the bar that summer, always sitting up at the counter, and always accompanied by his Jack Russell dog.

By 2005, I was fully aware that there was a lighthouse on Skellig Michael. I found myself wondering if it would be possible to see if I could spend a night out there. People did occasionally stay on the rock, archaeologists, for instance, and presumably others who were involved in maintenance, although I was vague as to who those others might be.

On 7 February 2005, I sent an email to the Commissioners of Irish Lights, explaining my project. I enquired if those who maintained the light at Skellig Michael ever stayed overnight and, if so, might it be possible for me to accompany them? I'm ashamed to report I didn't even have a name. I just sent it to their generic email address, a version of tossing a message in a bottle into the ocean, and prepared to wait weeks for it to be answered. It would have been easy to pick up the phone and find out the name of the person I needed to contact but, in some way, I didn't want an answer; I didn't want to get the no I expected.

To my incredulity, I had a reply the following day, from David Bedlow, the then Inspector of Lights and Marine Superintendent.

We have a maintenance visit on Skelligs Lighthouse planned for April. The maintenance team will live at the lighthouse. There is plenty of room at Skelligs Lighthouse and you could stay there too, subject to certain conditions.

Transport to the rock is by helicopter from Castletownbere, Co. Cork. If there is spare capacity in the helicopter, you could avail of it to fly to the rock, or you could make your own transport arrangements to travel to the rock by local boat for part of the time – irrespective of how you decide to travel, the journey will be subject to weather, sea conditions and other exigencies.

And there were details about writing a formal letter at least one month in advance, should I decide to go, and who to send it to.

I sat at my desk in the office on Fleet Street that the *Irish Times* then occupied and stared at my computer screen in a daze for a few minutes. Then I texted my older brother to tell him I had been offered a trip to Skelligs. Both my brothers had worked for John O' when they were teenagers, skippering tourists in *L'Oursin* out to Skelligs. On these runs, they used to bring out milk, newspapers and some perishable groceries for the lighthouse keepers.

Arthur replied: *Oh, you must go. Think of those monks and what they thought about each morning.*

But it was not the monks in their beehive huts, deep in past centuries, whom I was thinking of. It was the lighthouse keepers of 160 years who had lived there and manned the lights until so recently, these modern monks about whom Tony Parker had written so powerfully.

In the days that followed, to my astonishment, both my

brothers asked if they could come with me to Skelligs. Neither had ever shown the smallest interest in any writing project I had ever undertaken before. It was, of course, Skellig Michael that was luring them and the prospect of spending a night in the lighthouse there. For all the summers they had spent skippering tourists out to the rock, they had never been there overnight.

In the end, I wrote formally to the Commissioners of Irish Lights, asking if my brothers could join me. There was only one space in the helicopter, but they were planning to arrive by boat. My brother David lived in Bunavalla and was one of the volunteer members of the Derrynane Inshore lifeboat team. Their boat had to be regularly taken on training runs, and one of these could be to Skellig Michael.

The answer to my letter came back a week later: we could all go.

> You will need to bring your own food, drinking water and bedding. Everyone fends for themselves at a lighthouse.

It was 2005, but that evocative sentence could have come from half a century earlier: everyone fends for themselves at a lighthouse.

The basic pay at the time Parker was doing his research was £20 a week for a SAK; £21 a week plus a free house for an AK; and £25.50 plus a free house for a PK. Everyone also got paid an additional daily allowance for being on a rock or tower light, which was either 48 pence a day for a rock light or 60 pence a day for a tower light, plus 60 pence a day 'victualling' money, to cover their food. In 1974, when Parker was writing this book, the average weekly wage for a man in full-time manual employment was £48.63, so all lighthouse keepers, no matter what their status, were earning well below the average wage.

Back at shore, where Margaret, wife of Principal Keeper Stanley, was living, there were four cottages for the keepers of the rock lights. There was always one keeper at home on leave when the other three were 'off' at the rock. Parker talked to Paul, who was on his month ashore. He had learned how to make ships in bottles from Stanley, a craft he said lighthouse keepers originally learned to do as a way of making some extra money.

Paul was thirty and sanguine about the work he did. In the course of the narrative, it becomes clear that so much of the work involves unduly repetitive duties: polishing the polished brass handrails, endlessly washing already clean things, because there was so little else to do. Paul had been in the service long enough to know that most men who enter it never leave, because, or so he believed, there was nothing else they could do. He wondered with prescience what the point of a lighthouse keeper's job is, other than to keep the light going. What, he wondered, are they being paid for? 'For being there, that's all, I suppose.'

There is so much irony in the fact that almost all of the men Parker interviewed stated that they stayed in the job, even though they often hated it, because it offered security and certain employment for life. Within two decades of that interview with Paul, most lighthouses had been automated; computers, not men, would now keep the lights going. If Paul had stayed in the service, he would have been in his early fifties by the time the last lighthouses in Britain were automated, on

26 November in 1998, and still some years off retirement. What happened to men like him afterwards, and the other men who spent their whole lives working as lighthouse keepers?

But for me, the most poignant interview in the whole book was with Alf, the Assistant Keeper stationed on the same rock light as Stanley. Prior to his agreement to sit down with Parker for an interview, Alf was an elusive character. Nobody, either on land or at sea, was certain where he went on his month ashore. They just knew he was unmarried, did not have children and always turned up for duty at the very last minute.

Parker's method, once he was on a rock or a tower light, was to let the keepers decide if and when they wanted to talk to him in a one-on-one interview. Alf decided to do his interview at one in the morning, when he was on what was called the 'middle watch' of the day.

He was forty-nine at the time of the interview and told Parker he was one of eight children. His father died when he was four, his mother when he was twelve, and then the family were split up. He left school at fourteen and went to work in a factory. Thereafter, he spent all his wages on drink, lurching from job to job, until he joined the lighthouse service at thirty.

Then he left it ten years later, to try to set up a newsagent's in Leeds. He told Parker he had thought that because he managed without drinking while 'off' for eight weeks at a time he could manage full time in a 'normal' life without drinking. Six months later, Alf was destitute and living as a rough sleeper between the streets and a Salvation Army hostel. 'You couldn't say I was anything else than a down-and-out tramp.'

It was a chance encounter with a keeper he had formerly known that persuaded him to return to the lighthouse service and the austere security it provided. It's already become horribly clear to the reader that Alf remained an alcoholic who went cold turkey every time he came to the rock. He threw up every time on the journey out and could not eat for days on arrival, but it was not seasickness he suffered from.

Alf told Parker with a kind of heartbreaking cheeriness that he had been 'two different men so long now'. His first drink when he left the rock was at the train station en route to his digs. On his month off, he lived in digs with a landlady in Manchester. They had an arrangement that when his pay came through she took for his keep for the four weeks he was there, plus a bit extra to keep the room when he was away. Every other penny, he admitted, he spent on drink, rotating every day, all day, between the five pubs closest to his lodgings.

'It's not the companionship I go in for, only the drink,' he told Parker, saying he hardly ever talked to anyone when he was away from the rock. He had been lonely so long in his civilian life he no longer knew what companionship was.

But on the rock, and when in the company of the other two men he worked with, he said he was never lonely. He brought books and newspapers out to the lighthouse. He bought old clocks and took them apart to mend, then sold them in an antique shop in Manchester. He read Greek myths and history books and Shakespeare for pleasure. Once he had read something, it always stuck in his mind, he told Parker, not realizing how clever he was, although the reader does. 'I know things, all sorts of things, but they're bits and pieces with no rhyme or reason to them.'

The title of the chapter featuring Alf's interview is 'The Candle'. He talked about his personal philosophy, although he didn't use that word; he told Parker he once read something about how there were two ways of looking at a life. That life is darkness but that some people have a box of matches and others have a candle. The people who have the matches light them now and then and briefly see what things look like before the match goes out. The other people always have a candle to look at and, even if something gets in the way of the light now and then, the candle itself is always there.

Alf said that if he hadn't come back to the lighthouse service, he'd have been dead by now. That his 'proper life' was out on this rock light, where it was clean and fresh. That his life on shore was in the darkness, where there were no matches, but as long as he had the candle of the rock light and his job to come back to he would be OK.

These stories of Alf and Stanley and Paul and all the others have haunted me for years. Parker draws their characters so beautifully, with empathy and kindness and a total lack of judgement. Their voices have such authenticity.

What happened to Alf? It's his story in particular I can never forget, a story like a Greek myth. He is both unknowingly wise and knowingly doomed by fate; at some point, he would have had to retire from lighthouse service and the structure and refuge it provided. What happened to Alf then? I don't want to know, but I can guess with dread.

When I first read *Lighthouse*, somewhere within me I was afraid that I would become Alf. His story terrified me, that almost inevitable topple into some chasm of life chaos and the painful, excruciating scramble to get out of it. I don't know why a young woman of twenty-one would fear turning into a deeply damaged person more than twice her age.

But back then, when I didn't have many friends, I knew what being lonely was and how powerful and huge and overwhelming loneliness could be. I was afraid that loneliness might lead me to a life chaos similar to that of the man who seemed to stay alive only because he worked on a lighthouse on a rock surrounded by water, cut off from the world he could not survive long in.

On the morning of 13 April 2005, I flew to Skellig Michael on the helicopter with the maintenance crew. The maintenance trip had been shortened from a week to two days. The plan was that I was to stay for both nights. Regarding my brothers, who were coming in that afternoon on the rescue boat, Arthur was to also stay for two nights, and David one. The boat would come back for them.

There is something pleasingly subversive and thrilling about going through gates that have signs with 'No Admittance' on them. One of the three-person crew unlocked a series of gates along the path that led to the lighthouse.

No Admittance. By Order, Secretary, Commissioners of Irish Lights, Dublin

Their kit was transported in a wheelbarrow from the helipad, a circular piece of concrete on stilts, located close to the vertical rock face. I followed with my rucksack, which had my sleeping bag and some food in it; my brothers were bringing more provisions out with them in the boat. We did not, in the end, need fresh water; there was a supply at the lighthouse.

The lighthouse and cottages were built high up into a rock face; the elevation was fifty-three metres. At the cottages, the crew had their own living room and kitchen. There was a guest living room and kitchen, a bathroom, telephone room and control room; all downstairs. From every room, the sound of the ocean was audible. Upstairs were six small bedrooms. It was April, but still chill, and the place had that atmosphere places have when they haven't been occupied for some time, of trapped air and an accentuated smell of wood.

The bedroom I chose overlooked Seal Cove, the deep, wild bay that separates the headlands where the old upper lighthouse was located out of sight and this lower one. I went straight to the sash window. It framed a stunning and improbable view of sheer rock face directly opposite, dark blue ocean fringed with white foam far below. I felt a sensation of vertigo. I was looking down at the ocean from a great height, as high as the fulmars and guillemots that swooped past the window. More birds crowded together on distant rock ledges like avian white pearls on an uncertain string.

What lighthouse keepers of old had looked out of this window and seen this view? Did they even notice it any more after a while? I pulled down the window and leaned out into the wind. There was salt on the air, carried high up from the breaking waves and foam and spume that churned ceaselessly below.

My brothers arrived into Blind Man's Cove by boat in the afternoon. It was not often the three of us were together, and almost never as just the three of us. Although I had organized the trip, I fell back into the default hierarchal role of youngest: the Supernumerary Assistant Keeper dogsbody. My brothers were nine and seven years older than me. Both knew far more about life at sea than I did; David worked full time on a fish farm. They knew how to skipper boats and read the weather and tie knots; to do practical, useful and necessary maritime tasks that I knew nothing about. David had his two-way VHF marine radio with him. He was definitely Principal Keeper.

On the wall at the back of the lighthouse, there were a number of carvings of initials and names, some very beautifully done.

'Lighthouse keepers. It was a tradition to leave your name behind,' Richard Foran, one of the crew members, said, when I asked what they were.

We looked at them together. *J. O'Connor 1833. J. B. Donovan 1874. B. R. Jeffers 1888. D. P. Sullivan 1941. W. J. Hamilton.*

'I knew Hamilton,' Richard said. 'He was here in the 1930s. He made his own false teeth from the ivory handles of knives.'

In the late afternoon, my brothers and I made our way up the hundreds of stone steps to the beehive huts on the apex of Skelligs. Richard had told us that the men who had built the lighthouses back in the 1820s lived in the huts while they were working on the rock.

'They whitewashed them inside to make them brighter. If you look, you can still see some of it at the back of the stones,' he said.

But we had forgotten to bring torches and it was so dim inside it was impossible to see.

At the top, we wandered about, comparing notes as to how long it was since we had each been there. For me, it was seventeen years, for Arthur eight, and for David, although he had skippered boats out to the rock many, many times, it had been a quarter-century since he had actually climbed up to the top, where the beehive huts were.

Back at the cottages, the crew kept to their own quarters, their own kitchen and living room. We were to hardly see them for the duration of our stay, even though we were all under the one roof.

That first night, the three of us drank wine – something the lighthouse keepers of old definitely never did, as alcohol was forbidden at stations – and ate all of the delicious curry my sister-in-law had sent out. When I looked in the cupboards for china, I found a blue-rimmed side plate with a faded logo on it in blue. On the back was 'Arklow, made in the Republic of Ireland'. It was an old Arklow Pottery plate, a pottery that started up in 1934, was bought by a Japanese company in 1977 and has long since gone out of business. 'Irish Lighthouse Service' read a little banner over a drawing of a lighthouse, a ship and rocks. Under the drawing were the words '*In salutem omnium*'.

'For the safety of all,' Arthur translated.

A new moon shone through my window that night. I fell asleep, listening to the sounds of the waves far below.

At the time Parker was doing his research in the early 1970s, men still spent eight weeks off and then four weeks ashore. It would soon change to four weeks on duty and four weeks on leave; the psychological impact of being in tiny quarters with two other men not your family nor sometimes even your friends for months at a time must on occasion have been unspeakably awful.

Also, while land lights had the advantage of your family on-site and rock lights had enough space for each man to have his own bedroom, at tower lights, the challenges were many. There is one drawing in *Lighthouse*, a cross-section of a tower light. Servicemen were winched from the boat into the tower and on to the entrance floor that was many metres above sea level. The three rooms above the entrance were storerooms and, above those, all on separate floors, were the kitchen, bedroom, sitting room, service room and the lighthouse lens.

Parker, who spent some weeks at a tower light, explains that a spiral staircase ran around the inside wall, with the staircase between the rooms and the outer walls. Down the spine of the tower ran a 'weight tube', a mechanism on chains that once used to power the lenses, until it was replaced by electricity. While the weights were gone, the tube remained, and thus every room was shaped like a Polo mint.

The men living in this tower had curved bunks that hug the curved wall like bananas, as there is not enough room in the space for ordinary beds. The urinal was an old half-pint pewter mug on a window ledge outside the bedroom, which got emptied out the window after each use. It was the job of the dogsbody Supernumerary Assistant Keeper to empty the contents of the Elsan portable toilet off the railed gallery at the top of the lighthouse. In those long-off days when people cared a whole lot less about pollution, the sea was their dump. Parker reports that when the rubbish bin got full with scraps and tins, the contents were emptied on to newspapers, wrapped up, weighted with rocks and thrown into the ocean.

Rereading *Lighthouse*, I found myself even more gripped than I had been first time around. I had been absolutely enthralled in 1987 by the world Parker documented so carefully and, all these years later, it remains the best non-fiction book I've ever read. This time, I could see how skilled Tony Parker's process had been. The care and thought and time he put into this one book was staggering.

There are layers and layers of subtlety to the text, in all its many perspectives. He himself is watermarked into the narrative because it is his point of view that shapes it all, along with his masterful editing.

*

By morning on Skelligs, the waves were much, much louder. It was a bright, cold, sunny day, but the wind was howling past my window.

It was, in fact, blowing such a gale that David soon discovered over breakfast via his VHF radio that the boat would not put to sea that day to take him off. He was due at work that afternoon, but the weather had other plans.

'Good thing we brought some extra grub,' he said.

We eyed our remaining supplies. Three tins of beans. Three tins of vegetable soup. Three tins of tuna. Three Mars bars. A piece of cheese. Most of a loaf of brown bread. A jar of chutney.

This was what we shared out between us over the next two days because, as it turned out, the following day was even more stormy. Not only could the boat not launch from Derrynane two days in a row, Richard went to the helipad and declared the wind conditions too dangerous for a helicopter landing. We would be spending an unscheduled third night at the lighthouse.

On that third day, I think I understood a bit of what it must have been like to be out there on the lighthouse, day after day, night after night – the ennui of it. The first day had been all novelty. Like the keepers of old, we ate all the fresh food first and then had to switch to tins and endless mugs of tea. The three of us scattered during the day. Arthur alternated between going up to the beehive huts by himself with his camera and lying in the sleeping bag in his room, dozing. David was on his VHF radio or pacing the paths between the lighthouse and Blind Man's Cove or reading in the living room.

Although it was blowing a gale, it was sunny, and I took a book up to the beehive huts both afternoons, fell asleep in the sea campion and woke up as the puffins were flying back in from their day out at sea, while their mates waddled out of burrows to await them. I wrote my diary. I ran my fingers over the deep carvings of the names of the former lighthouse keepers. How had those trios of three men coped, cooped up together for weeks at a time, in a tower light, where you could not go outside and had not a shred of privacy? I felt a bit dazed, as if I was in and out of time.

The three of us gathered together in the evening for our ever more frugal meals. It remains the longest period of time we have spent together in our adult lives; just us. We didn't have deep conversations, or discuss philosophical thoughts, or talk about anything personal. I had vaguely thought being together at the lighthouse might prompt such exchanges but, of course, I had been romanticizing things in my head again. I get on perfectly fine with my brothers; we just don't tend to have those kinds of conversations in ordinary circumstances, so we were hardly likely to have them because we happened to be around a table at a stormbound lighthouse far out on a rock in the Atlantic.

We talked instead about the weather forecast and our dwindling food supply and reverted to childhood nicknames for each other. My brothers went outside every now and then to smoke. They were far more concerned about running out of cigarettes and tobacco than food.

On the morning of the fourth day, the wind finally dropped. We packed up our stuff and I looked out my bedroom window one last time.

The rescue boat came out for my brothers first. The crew closed up the lighthouse and locked the gates again, and we went to the helipad together to wait for the helicopter we could see in the distance flying steadily towards us.

*

Rereading *Lighthouse,* I wondered more and more what had happened to the tapes and where Tony Parker's astonishing archive of bygone social history is now. So I began to google. There is not much out there, but I did find a BBC Radio 4 documentary first broadcast in 2012 called *The Great Listener.* It was made by historian Alan Dein, who met Parker just once, when he conducted a live interview with him at the National Film Theatre in London. The documentary draws on archival recordings held by the BBC, including extracts of interviews with Parker himself.

'I usually try and sit on a slightly lower level than the person I'm talking to, so you don't get the sense of literally talking down to somebody,' are the first words you hear from Parker. His slightly sing-song voice is musical and measured, calm and unhurried. It's a voice that sounds kindly and also innately confident; this, I thought listening, is a person who knows he is in control. 'And I have the tape recorder very conspicuous and until we have got to the point where we don't look at the tape recorder any more, I don't think the interviewing starts properly.'

Dein describes Parker's interviewing style as 'audio martial arts'.

'His empathy was his driving force. He was able to enter into more lives than anyone else I've ever seen achieve,' documentary maker Roger Graef observes. 'Tony's silences were so eloquent that he was inviting people to talk.'

One of the people Dein interviews is Tim Parker, Tony Parker's son and the person to whom *Lighthouse* is dedicated. Tim Parker says he was a boy of fourteen at boarding school when his father was writing it. 'He used to do all the interviews on TDK ninety-minute cassettes. There would be 200 or 300 cassettes for each book, and I was always after them after he had finished using them,' he says. Tim explains he wanted the cassettes so he could record music over them.

Listening in my kitchen, I put a hand over my eyes. Had Parker's teenage son taped the chart hits of the 1970s over the voices of Alf, and Stanley and Margaret and Paul, and all the others?

It was worse.

'He would never, ever let me have them,' Tim says. 'So we had to have an incinerator at the bottom of the garden and, to my abject horror, it was my job to take these two or three hundred cassette tapes and burn the lot of them.'

My rereading of *Lighthouse* was during Ireland's second lockdown. I'm older now than Alf was when he was interviewed by Parker. My life to date has mercifully not – and I hope never will – involved destitution, addiction or social isolation. But it has included lacunas of loneliness.

Perhaps the book speaks to me so powerfully again not only for the lost community it documents but because it is at core such a nuanced story of enforced isolation and loneliness. I identified with that loneliness. Living alone during lockdown is the nearest I'll ever get, or want to get, to being far out on a tower light in the Atlantic.

During that time, my friends were as far away as the unnavigable shoreline, no matter how often we talked on screen. Our video calls and the reminder of our geographical and physical distance were sometimes as unhelpful to me as Margaret's Sunday circumnavigation of Stanley's island light, when she waved at him and he was left not in solace but stricken, wanting to swim back to shore. Sometimes when I ended those lockdown video calls, I cried alone in my house, the house that had become a virtual lighthouse where I was Principal Keeper, Assistant Keeper and Supernumerary Assistant Keeper all in one.

I had to keep believing that this time of enforced isolation would end, that someday lockdown would be over and a boat would arrive to winch me out of my sea-bound tower and convey me to my real life. I thought again of what Alf had said all those years ago to Tony Parker, about life being darkness, that some people have only a box of matches to illuminate it and others only a candle. But I don't believe that. I believe you can have both. And I believe that if the candle gets blown out, then you can always light it again.

Choices: The Portrait of a Lady, by Henry James (1881)

One of the big books back in 2004 was Colm Tóibín's *The Master*. It was a beautiful and compelling imagined re-creation of four key years in the life of the novelist Henry James. After I had read it, I became extremely curious to read something by Henry James and hear the original Jamesian voice; he was a writer of whom I had never before read anything.

I was browsing in a charity shop not long after finishing *The Master* and came across a second-hand copy of *The Portrait of a Lady*. The name of the previous owner was written in blue biro on the flyleaf: Gary Keena. I paid a euro for Gary Keena's former book and brought it home with me. One evening, I picked it up from the pile beside my bed and decided to read a couple of chapters before going to sleep.

Hours later, I turned off the light, my mind afire. I was

more than a third of the way through its 600 pages and was both absolutely gripped and shaken. Isabel Archer's story seemed so modern to me; her story seemed so personal, as did her dilemmas. Her story spoke to me more powerfully than any other I had ever read.

I stumbled through work the following day, stupid from lack of sleep, dazed and troubled by what I had read the previous night. All I could think of that day was getting back to the book that had been written 123 years previously. As soon as I got home, I snatched it up again. How could Henry James have understood so much about human life? I marvelled. How had he known all this? Would he ever have guessed that at least one woman reading his novel more than a century later would recognize elements of her own life story within it?

Again, I read for hours. The expression 'page-turner' is tossed around a lot in literature. It usually refers to the excitement of thrillers and tightly plotted crime novels. I had read plenty of these kinds of books, racing through their pages, driven on by the plot. That night, I read a Victorian novel with similar adrenaline.

Not long after 3 a.m., I finished the book. My mind was in turmoil. I felt overwhelmed in many ways. A terrible realization had come upon me. I saw so clearly my own mistakes in those Isabel Archer had made, the mistakes she had made about choices. I remained awake until dawn, trying to process this insight I had just discovered.

It is not, I don't think, a spoiler to reveal plot elements of a book written more than a century ago. The core character is Isabel Archer, an American-born young woman whose wealthy and forthright aunt, Mrs Lydia Touchett, brings her to England after both her parents have died. Her two older sisters are married, but Isabel is not, although she leaves behind her a suitor, the wonderfully named Caspar Goodwood. Caspar is the heir to an industrial fortune. Isabel has virtually no financial means, but she possesses character, spirit, independence and a hunger for life, travel and experiences.

She comes to Gardencourt, the English estate bought by Daniel Touchett, the banker husband of Lydia Touchett. Isabel not only makes an immediate impression on her ill cousin, Ralph, but also on the Touchetts' neighbour, Lord Warburton, a smart, handsome and kind man of immense wealth.

A marriage proposal follows from Lord Warburton. Isabel more or less eats him for breakfast, so decisively does she turn him down. She refuses him not because she doesn't like him immensely but because she believes it is the wrong choice for her to make, that she would be surrendering her independence in doing so. 'Though she was lost in admiration of her opportunity she managed to move back into the deepest shade of it, even as some wild, caught creature in a vast cage.'

Isabel is also far from pleased to hear, soon after, that Caspar Goodwood has followed her to England in the hope that she will change her mind. She turns him down again. She wants more, even if she is not sure what that more is. More of a challenge. Something more difficult. Something less predictable.

In his preface, Henry James writes about the force that informs Isabel's character, that her character was 'bent upon its fates – some fate or other; which, among the possibilities, being precisely the question'.

Ralph, who also loves Isabel but knows he is a slowly dying man, wants to give her what he considers total freedom. Unknown to her, he persuades his father to change his will, thereby leaving Isabel a staggering fortune of £70,000. Ralph believes that money will give Isabel true independence and freedom, freedom to make her own choices in marriage. Having no need of money, she can now do as she wishes. She can choose not to marry at all or marry anyone she pleases for love, not simply money, because she has plenty of her own. These opportunities and choices are what Ralph hopes to create for Isabel by intervening in her fate.

I used an inflation converter I found on the British National Archives website to compare the value of the sum of £70,000 in 1880 to the modern-day equivalent. It came up with a sum over £4.5 million, a fortune indeed, even by today's standards.

But Isabel's new fortune inevitably makes her a target. What happens is that she is slowly coerced into a terrible marriage by the odious, stone-cold Gilbert Osmond, who is interested only in her money. She is gradually drawn into it with such psychological subtlety and dexterity that she does not realize she is not, in fact, making either a free or a correct choice. Isabel falsely believes him to be a man of independence and impeccable taste, of high ideas and ideals and all the more admirable for not caring that he lives by modest means. The truth is, she has no idea what he is really like, whereas Gilbert identifies at once what he wants to quell in her character, nothing less than the essence of her spirit: 'too many ideas . . . fortunately, they're very bad ones'.

Isabel ignores both her own true instincts and the advice of those who truly love her. She sees Gilbert as noble, as unconventional, like her, as a choice of partner contradictory to what society might have expected of the marriage partner of a wealthy young woman. Marrying him is the challenge she believes she seeks, a counter-intuitive choice. Ralph – who sees Gilbert Osmond exactly for the calculating narcissist he is – realizes what is happening, but it is too late. Isabel is coldly offended by his efforts to intervene. The marriage of Isabel to Gilbert is to be one, as Mrs Touchett presciently describes it, 'of morbid perversity'.

That is exactly what happens, and it is not long before it becomes pitifully evident to Isabel. Two thirds of the way through the novel, she reflects on her disastrous marriage. 'The sole source of her mistake had been within herself. There had been no plot, no snare; she had looked and considered and chosen.'

It was this, the fact Isabel admitted to herself that she was responsible for the choice she had made, responsible for a choice that was a mistake; it was this that stunned me to the point that I was actually shaking that night when I stayed up late reading Henry James's novel.

I, too, like Isabel Archer, had made wrong choices. Sometimes with my relationships and often with other things in life. I, like her, had made the mistake of thinking that because one choice seemed the easy one to make it was thus the lesser option. The wrong option. The less challenging option. But I had not understood, until I read *The Portrait of a Lady*, that sometimes what seems like the easy option is in fact the right choice. It's easy because it is obviously right. What is not right is to automatically choose the more difficult option every single time, because – as I believed then – it shows more character to be constantly challenging oneself.

I sat in my house that night and thought about some of the times I had chosen to make my life so unnecessarily hard for myself. The first one that came into my head, because it was something I had uneasily thought about from time to time over the years, was that time in Kathmandu, back in 1994.

That time when I chose not to take a rickshaw back to my guest house late at night from outside the Yak and Yeti Hotel, where I had gone to meet other backpackers for drinks.

Instead, I waved the waiting rickshaw away. I was an independent woman, unafraid of walking home alone in the darkness, and I was not going to get into that rickshaw and cop out of walking home. Kathmandu was very safe and I knew my way around the streets after weeks there.

What happened that night was not an attack from any person but from three wild street dogs, who came for me, howling out of nowhere in a ferocious, circling pack as I turned the corner on to the street where my guest house was located. The terror I felt while alone that night, the helplessness and panic, the fear I felt after I was bitten – because bitten I was – and the long series of rabies shots I had to have afterwards: all these things could have been avoided if I had been less stubborn with myself. If I had made a better choice that night and taken the rickshaw that would have left me at the door and waited until I was inside, a choice that was better because it was the right choice, the choice I had yet again automatically dismissed as being too easy.

I sat up all night in my house that night, *The Portrait of a Lady* beside me, and realized with painful clarity that the foundations on which I had built so much of my life were faulty. The Kathmandu episode was a kind of symbol for all the other poor choices I had consciously made. There had been so many other times in my life when I had made terrible decisions: chiefly about romantic relationships but also about jobs and all kinds of opportunities, because I inevitably scorned the 'easy' choice when making decisions. I mistakenly thought that in making these decisions, in choosing the difficult choice, I was being true to myself. But who, except myself, was ever policing my choices? Nobody had forced me into them. The sole source of my mistakes had been within myself, as Isabel Archer's had been.

That night, I realized I was in possession of a seismic, life-changing piece of knowledge. What I now did with it was up to me.

The year I lived in Cambridge, Massachusetts, I passed William James Hall on Kirkland Street almost every day. William and Henry were brothers, who had both attended Harvard, and William was equally famous, a revered philosopher and psychologist. The tall landmark building that carries his name in a campus of landmark buildings was designed by Minoru Yamasaki, who also designed the ill-fated World Trade Center in New York.

As I traversed the streets of Cambridge that year, I kept looking for a plaque to show me where the James family had lived. There were so many plaques all over Cambridge, but I could never find one that told me where their house had been. One afternoon, when I was sitting in the bar of the Faculty Club on Quincy Street, waiting for my Hanger Sisters to show up, I leafed through the book I had just bought in the Coop. It was a kind of trivia guide to the university, a Harvard A–Z.

As I was right then actually sitting in the Faculty Club, I looked up the entry for it in the F section. The first sentence read: 'The club's neo-Georgian building stands on a Quincy Street plot where Henry James Sr and his notable family once lived.' I had been in the Faculty Club many times but now I looked around me with amazement, as if I was seeing it for the first time. These were the views they saw through the window. This was the very piece of land on which they had lived out their domestic lives. It was here, located somewhere in the air directly above me, that Henry James had lain in his bed at night and dreamed.

On my last full day in Cambridge in June 2009, I had one final mission to complete. My bags were packed. I had said goodbye to all my haunts. But there was one specific place I had not yet been, a place I had been keeping until the very end of my time, a pilgrimage I had waited ten months to make.

That afternoon, I bought yellow roses at the florist's on Brattle Square. Then I walked to Cambridge Cemetery, where I knew the James family plot was located. It took perhaps half an hour of walking above the buried dead to find it. There is a row of six headstones in front of an oblong red-brick wall on Meadow Avenue. William's grave is the second of the six and Henry's is the fifth.

Henry James's epitaph reads: *Novelist – citizen of two countries. Interpreter of his generation on both sides of the sea.*

Ever since reading *The Portrait of a Lady,* I have tried very hard to adjust my previous default setting of always opting for the most difficult choices. It's hard to reverse the habit of a lifetime, but it's possible. I still make some terrible choices, but at least I think about them properly now. My life has changed for the better as a result, and it's a book I have to thank for that, and a writer who has now been dead for over a century.

I laid my roses on the grass in front of his headstone and thought again about Isabel Archer, whose character was *bent upon its fates – some fate or other*; which, *among the possibilities, being precisely the question.* The ending of the novel is deliberately ambiguous. We don't know what is next for Isabel, although I have my own theory as to how her life unfolded afterwards.

What I felt that June afternoon, standing beside Henry James's grave, was profound gratitude. He wrote a book that transformed my life, reached far into the future and helped someone from another era. It's a strange thing to know you have been upheld by someone dead long before you were born, as if the man who wrote one of literature's most famous ghost stories was himself a kind of sentient ghost.

I stood there for several minutes beside his grave, the yellow roses glowing in the June sunlight like molten gold.

ACKNOWLEDGEMENTS

Thank you to all my comrades who so generously allowed me to write about them in this book. Some of you asked to appear under different names, so I duly rechristened several of you.

Thank you very much also to these friends who helped, supported and encouraged me in countless different ways. Brian Leyden, Carmel Jennings, Charlie Connelly, Chris Delaney, Elayne Devlin, Ciara Higgins, Declan Jones, Deirdre Falvey, Derek Scally, Eileen Lyons, Ellen MacNally, Freya McClements, Giles Newington, Helen Comerford, Hilary Fannin, Hope Reese, Janet Pierce, Jennifer Bray, Jennifer O'Connell, Joseph Woods, Joyce Hickey, Jude Leavy, Katie Donovan, Madeleine Keane, Madeleine Moore, Marie-Claire Digby, Medb Lambert, Oliver Comerford, Oonagh Young, Patrick Freyne, Rosie Schaap, Sarah McCann, Susan Arnott, Tanya Sweeney, Tommy Tomlinson, Vincent Boland.

My family. Thank you to the Bolands, Corcorans and Blancs, including Amelie; and to Lara Morawiec, Giles Lord and Bertie.

Thank you to Fiona Murphy, editorial director at Transworld Ireland, and my editor on this book. I know how lucky I am to have you as my editor. Thanks also to Beci Kelly, Issy Hanrahan, Sharika Teelwah, Vivien Thompson, Sorcha Judge, Laura Dermody and Sophie Dwyer.

ABOUT THE AUTHOR

Rosita Boland is a senior features writer at the *Irish Times*, specializing in human interest stories. She was a 2009 Nieman Fellow at the Nieman Foundation for Journalism at Harvard University. She won 'Journalist of the Year' at the 2018 Newsbrands Ireland journalism awards. Her previous collection, *Elsewhere: One Woman, One Rucksack, One Lifetime of Travel*, was shortlisted for Non-Fiction Book of the Year at the An Post Irish Book Awards.